M000288118

WEALTH HABITS

SIX ORDINARY STEPS
TO ACHIEVE EXTRAORDINARY FINANCIAL FREEDOM

CANDY VALENTINO

WILEY

Library of Congress Cataloging-in-Publication Data is Available:
ISBN 9781394152292 (Cloth)
ISBN 9781394152308 (ePub)
ISBN 9781394152315 (ePDF)

Cover Design: Wiley
Cover Images: Author Photos Courtesy of the Author
Gold Foil: © phochi/Getty Images

SKY10036038_092622

Dedicated to rescue dogs everywhere, especially mine.

*Your unconditional love has always made
me feel like the richest person in the world.*

Contents

Wealth Habit 5
Investing Your Way to Wealth 175

Wealth Habit 6
Giving Your Way to Wealth 205

Introduction

Have you ever bought a book about money, personal finance, or wealth and realized that it's basically pep talk with no actual advice? Pages and pages are littered with the same basic motto of "Believe you'll make money, and you will!" over and over and over again.

You get through the first 70% of the book thinking, "Surely it will get better eventually" without it ever getting better? By the end of the book (if you get to the end), you realize there wasn't a drop of practical advice on how to make more money, how to keep more of what you make, or how to become financially free.

If that's you, I feel you.

"Think and get rich" will only take you so far. You also have to "*do* and get rich" to actually become wealthy and be financially free.

You can't sit on your couch and think "I'll have financial freedom, I'll become wealthy!" and not actually *do* anything about it.

You don't need another book filled with a bunch of regurgitated fluffy talking points to be convinced you should build wealth—you already want it. What you need to know is *how* to get there.

Wealth Habits teaches you just that—the habits anyone can develop and use to build real, lasting wealth.

There are dozens of great books out there that will give you motivation, inspiration, and encouragement. That's great if you want to be pumped up and motivated but don't want the actual steps to become wealthy and build financial freedom. *Wealth Habits* is your road map—a book of actionable steps to get off the hamster wheel of "work to pay bills" once and for all.

Your thoughts and beliefs about money *are* a part of building wealth, but it is not the *only* part. Chocolate chip cookies need chocolate chips, but that's not the only thing they need. It's simply one part of the recipe, and you still need other crucial ingredients.

Who Am I to Help You Build Wealth Habits?

There are loads of books written by authors with PhDs, MBAs, and all the other letters in the alphabet—I don't have any of those. I haven't studied a specific topic for the last 10 years. *I lived it*—for my entire life—and have been applying it on my own for more than 25 years.

I was 19 when I started my first business, but my life experience up until that point was growing up in a little white trailer with my two teenage parents in a rural, blue-collar town with a population of 2,000.

It goes without saying that I didn't have a rich family to teach me lessons about money and building wealth—yet I still found my way to being financially free. And that's the exact reason why I know that anyone who picks up this book—regardless of what's in your bank account, regardless of where you live, regardless of the family you grew up in, and regardless of your current circumstance in life—can build wealth too. That includes *you*!

I've built several multi-million dollar businesses and have bought, renovated, and flipped countless real estate properties in multiple states, acquired residential and commercial rental properties, and built a multi-million dollar real estate portfolio—with no money, no degree, no corporate background, and no rich parents.

So often I hear from people looking for some flashy "magic bullet" answer. I can see them wanting me to tell them the "one secret" that will unlock riches for them.

Here's the "one secret," the truth:

I didn't do anything extraordinary. I just did a lot of *ordinary* things. No magic bullet, no earth-shattering invention, no perfectly timed investment— just ordinary, normal things that *anyone* can do. Including **you**.

That's my secret to success, and it's the secret upon which this book is based.

What This book Is Really All About

This is not a flashy book. It's a *gritty* book. One that will teach you how to do those ordinary things really well to create, grow, and retain wealth over time. You can do the same by following the six proven *wealth habits* I developed and followed in my own ascent to wealth.

Here are a few things I'll cover as they relate to you creating financial freedom:

- How the BS you hear could be keeping you broke.
- How to develop multiple streams of income.
- How to build a real business—and make more money.
- How to pay less in taxes and keep more of what you make.
- How to score with the hat trick of real estate investing.
- How self-education pays financial dividends.
- How to protect your finances and your family.

- How to stop working and retire early—*and rich.*
- How to recession-proof your life—and your investments.
- How contribution creates real wealth—and the science behind it all.

Not only can you build wealth with these habits, but they are also crucial for protecting yourself, and your family, against the unavoidable twists and turns of economic and industry cycles.

One More Thing Before We Start: How to Best Use This Book

Before we begin, I want to give you a couple of tips on how to get the most out of this book. First, this isn't a book of concepts and ideas to ponder—it's a road map to creating financial freedom. The six *wealth habits* have separate steps and tools within each section and chapter. They can all be used together or can be followed separately.

There is going to be a lot of information, so if you don't quite get something on the first read through, reread that section or chapter because *repetition* is the secret to building any skill.

Wealth Habits is about your financial future, not your financial past. We will talk about all of the things to do now, not the things you did or didn't do. So if regret or shame pops up, drop them at the door so we can move forward toward the life you deserve.

For anyone who desires financial security and, ultimately, financial freedom—creating *wealth habits* is no longer a luxury. It's a necessity.

When you don't apply *wealth habits*, you run the financial risks that come from relying on the other (bad or ineffective) habits most Americans have that keeps them on a perpetual hamster wheel and, ultimately, broke.

These *wealth habits* are the not-so-obvious secrets of how the wealthy become—and stay—wealthy, which unfortunately isn't taught to the masses.

The good news is that it's not magic, it's not a secret, and it's not even complicated.

It's time to learn how to apply these *wealth habits* in your life and join the movement by taking control of your future and creating the financial freedom you deserve. Now let's get started!

WEALTH HABITS

WEALTH HABIT 1

Growing Your Way to Wealth

CHAPTER 1

How the BS You Hear Could Be Keeping You Broke

A s I said in the Introduction of this book, "Think and get rich" will only take you so far. You also have to *do and get rich* to actually become wealthy and be financially free.

Wealth Habits teaches you the tools to build real, lasting wealth, but you can't start the journey toward financial freedom if you are dragging around BS beliefs about money and wealth.

Which is why this chapter is first. I can give you all the action steps to get wealthy, but I'd be doing you a huge disservice if we don't address your thoughts and your inherent beliefs first because that is the driver to key financial decisions we make every day.

Increasing your financial intelligence can solve many of life's problems. Without this kind of knowledge we are doomed to repeat the pattern of "work to pay bills." And although there is a science to being wealthy, it first starts with an idea. An idea to change, an idea to stop running in the rat race, an idea to break through all of the BS passed down—or picked up—about money and start getting the education to build wealth.

But here's the thing, unless you grew up in a magical environment with wealthy parents who had financial wisdom—no one knows this stuff. So if you've ever beaten yourself up for making this decision or not making that decision—

"I shouldn't have sold that house."
"I should have bought that stock."
"I shouldn't have hired that person."
"I should have left that relationship sooner."
"I shouldn't have. . . I shouldn't have. . . I shouldn't have. . ."

—that stops today. You didn't know what you didn't know. And I get it. I was right there with you.

Growing up with blue collar, teenage parents, money was often scarce. And the conversation about financial literacy was nonexistent. I used to define "the rich" by anyone who had an upstairs to their house, a fireplace to hang Christmas stockings, or those who went on a beach vacation every summer.

I had a friend in school who I thought was the definition of "rich." Her house had an upstairs *and* a basement, she had an in-ground pool, and she took vacations with her whole family. Both of her parents had degrees—one was a teacher, the other was in sales—and her dad drove a new Cadillac. You get the gist.

But if you look at someone else with more money than you, and it makes you feel less in any way, you're getting caught in a scarcity mindset, which is a common, negative mindset about money. The perception that earning more or having more means that we have enough—or *are* enough—is a mindset even yours truly got caught up in my early 20's.

Achieving financial freedom will only come from seeing wealth for what it is—attainable. It is having the understanding that wealth is available to you, too, as it will never be attained from the fear of scarcity. Scarcity and lack holds you hostage to where you are and keeps you broke in the process.

When our basic needs are met (currently estimated at $75,000 a year), studies show that making more money doesn't buy incremental returns for living a satisfying life.

Regardless of how much money or how many possessions we have, the important part is how we relate to what we have—that is key in this first step.

Remember that which we *appreciate* and focus on grows. But that which we *fear* and focus on *also* grows. When our attention goes to what is lacking, we base our lives on the feelings of insufficiency, inadequacy, and incompleteness, and thus, we start to feel more of each.

We can set any amount of money in our heads—anywhere from $5,000 to $500,000—and imagine that if only we had that much more money—just that much more—*then* we would then have enough, be enough, and be happy. But we don't realize that we once thought the exact same thing when we had $5,000, $50,000, or even $500,000 *less* than we currently do now.

As another example, suppose we establish that if you received a 10% pay raise, or earned 10% more in your business, then you'd have enough to be cared for and comfortable. And abracadabra! Let's say you got that. Now imagine for a moment, that you find out that a coworker received a 25% pay raise or your friend who started in business at the same time as you increased their net income by 25%. All of a sudden, your 10% just isn't enough.

No one argues that more money can reduce problems or minimize the financial stress and anxiety in our lives. But approaching the pursuit of more wealth from a posture of scarcity can create more stresses or worsen existing issues. This type of negative emotional stacking can actually keep you *away* from building wealth.

If you've ever experienced money-related stress—about the aspects of *earning, giving, spending, saving,* or *losing it*—you need to carefully examine the beliefs you have and take a look at your overall approach to money.

The key to a healthier, more successful approach is to appreciate what you have, *while* going after that which you truly desire. The way to live a truly rich life is by finding the intersection of appreciation and ambition.

Your Brain Is not Pre-Wired for Happiness, Abundance or Wealth; It's Your Job to Re-Wire It.

The good news is you get to choose which emotions you want to experience the most. And because your unconscious beliefs drive your emotions, you first need to address the beliefs you have about money (Team Tony, n.d).

If you feel anxious around money now, you're always going to feel that way—no matter your success, how much money you make, or how much wealth you create.

Abundance is a mindset, a belief, a chosen perspective—it's not a dollar amount. Cultivate gratitude for what you have now, and everything you achieve will feel like an immense bonus. The truth of the matter is that more than 75% of the world lives on $2 a day. Your worst nightmare is their greatest possible dream.

Lack of appreciation for what you already have is the one thing that will not only make you truly poor, but it will keep you there.

Unconscious beliefs about money and the wealth habits you lack will ultimately keep you from the life you want.

There is science-backed proof of how the mind plays a role in your wealth and in your overall financial future. And this book wouldn't be complete without addressing its role in the big picture of building wealth habits. However, it's only part of it.

Online marketing and social media are full of coaches, gurus, and marketers talking about "money mindset" and "visualizing your abundant future." All the while they rent instead of owning their house, just started their first business, or haven't built any assets. So, although this book is certainly not about money mindset—and more about the real tactics that create financial wealth and financial freedom—I would fail you and your goals if I didn't include it, because it does matter.

A Poor Mentality Will Give You a Broke Reality

I believe it was Jim Rohn who said, "You are the sum of the five people you hang out with." So if you hang out with the Negative Nancies and Broke Bobs of the world, if you are friends with gossiping or broke people—those who live beyond their means and don't invest in themselves by building wealth habits—you too will end up adopting those behaviors.

Part of growing your bank account requires you to grow your mindset, change your beliefs, and develop new habits. I've worked with thousands of people, spent thousands of hours reading and researching, and it is undeniable the science and psychology of how your finances and the money that you have are directly related to your thoughts and emotions around them.

What you think about money, how you think about people with money, and the emotions you have tied to money will be a subconscious driver either toward or away from what you desire.

It is worth spending some time to become aware of the thoughts and the emotions directly tied to money for you because without self-awareness, your subconscious wiring will override your conscious desires and rational thinking, and those old thoughts and beliefs (which aren't serving you) will end up driving your actions, behaviors, and habits.

And here's the deal, there's no shame here. You're not alone. This is a huge piece for a lot of people. Some of the common fears around money are not having enough, looking stupid, appearing greedy, being exposed, and having guilt or even shame. You might feel guilty because you have more than your friends, or guilty that your money came too easily, or guilty that you desire more. You could feel shame realizing you avoid your finances, you spend too much, you buy stuff when you're unhappy, or that you simply don't have enough.

Negative emotions around money is something that needs to be addressed and changed because it creates a vicious, unconscious cycle that no matter how many of these wealth habits you practice, if you don't fix the negative, you'll keep coming back to those emotions, thoughts, and feelings around money, and it will sabotage your efforts.

Here's how it unfolds. Let's say you're sitting down and taking a hard look at your financial situation, and you're starting to create an investment plan. Just thinking about this increases your anxiety because you're afraid you're not going to face the reality, or you have nowhere near enough saved, or you're spending far too much. That anxiety then leads you to avoidance. You postpone it, you delay, you distract yourself with some shiny object in the moment, and then, because you're distracted and postponed the task, your anxiety drops, which then gives you a positive reinforcement for the avoidance of the behavior. And then you repeat this cycle over and over, instead of doing what you know you need to do.

The only way to break the pattern is to confront the dreaded task. You are stronger than the whims of your brain—know that. The way to break through is to continue to face the facts and move forward with the task. Your anxiety will temporarily increase. However, if you stay with it, it will steadily decline. You have to tolerate the short term pain to achieve long term gain.

No matter the family you grew up in, every family has its own psychology of money. What is talked about, what shouldn't be talked about, who is in control of the money, what responsibilities are assigned to whom. How important money is, what thoughts and beliefs they have about money or people who have money. The subject of money is where your family and childhood influences never end, until *you* end them.

Money stories are always a part of a family's identity, whether conscious or unconscious. Perhaps your father had a bad business deal and almost lost everything. Perhaps your mother was a brilliant businesswoman and her ideas were stolen, which then caused her to be cheated out of her financial freedom. Their beliefs and habits already exist, and they've been passed down to you. The goal is to identify the beliefs you have, and see if they're giving you the financial future you want. If they aren't, we're going to change them.

Regardless of what negative associations you've learned about money (and yes, they have all been learned), here's the truth: Money simply magnifies a person's virtues and flaws. So if you are a greedy, immoral person, obtaining wealth will magnify those bad traits. But if you're a good person, an honest, caring, and giving person—money will magnify those traits and give you the ability to help more people.

> **Money is simply something you exchange. Money is replaceable and replenishable.**

Here is a scientific fact about money:

You can rewire your brain and choose a different script about how you think of money. Not figuratively, literally. *While most of the neurons in our brain have been with us since birth, and age does take a toll, our brains still make new neurons. This process is known as neurogenesis.*

As reported in *Scientific American*, a 2019 study published by the journal *Nature Medicine* looked at the brain tissue of 58 recently deceased people and found that the adult brain can indeed generate new neurons (Weintraub, 2019). Your cells in your body are also constantly replaced and made new. In fact, our entire body, every cell in our entire body, is new every six months, which means you can change your beliefs, your thoughts, or your body based on your habits and develop an entirely different structure. Your brain can rewire itself. Neuroplasticity, or the brain's ability to recognize and change itself throughout a person's lifetime, is a truly remarkable thing.

Research published in the journal *Nature Neuroscience* suggests a person's brain activity is as unique as their own fingerprints. To reach their conclusion, scientists used functional magnetic resonance imaging (FMRI) to create connectivity profiles, which allowed researchers to identify the brain activity of more than a hundred individuals (Finn *et al*, 2015). Learning about individual brain connections offered scientists incredible insights.

There is science, real data, that proves: regardless of what you've been told, regardless of the amount of debt you have or the income you currently make—you too can use wealth habits and change your financial future.

Now let's get to the next step. . .

CHAPTER 2

Four Common Beliefs Keeping You Broke

Throughout this book, we'll be addressing the very tactical, tangible steps of wealth building, and I'll be sharing the specific necessary and actionable steps that lead to financial freedom.

Of course, there are lots of tangible reasons that keep you broke—overspending, not investing, racking up bad debt on depreciating assets—and you may be aware of those. But there are many intangible habits that come into play as well.

I can teach you all the tangible steps that will make you wealthy, but if we don't address a few of the intangible beliefs most people carry around with them, we'll be swimming upstream together.

The faster we break these beliefs, the sooner we can get on our way to building the *wealth habits*. So let's jump into it.

There are four common beliefs keeping you broke:

Broke Belief #1: Scarcity

Scarcity is a belief that wealth is limited, that you can run out of money or will never have enough. The term "scarcity mindset" was coined by the author Stephen Covey in his book *The 7 Habits of Highly Effective People*.

As discussed in a recent *Business Insider* article, "There are two main facets: the thought that wealth and opportunities are limited, and the fear that one will never have enough. A scarcity mindset can also come with an obsession with what one is lacking. This creates a tunnel vision of sorts, making it more difficult to move forward and achieve financial goals" (Yale, 2022). The article continues, "the opposite of a scarcity mindset is an abundance mindset—the view that there is limitless wealth and opportunity in the world" (Stinson, 2019).

You can overcome the scarcity mindset and shift your perspective to abundance by making small, daily changes.

1. **Build Your Knowledge**

   Learning more and expanding your knowledge about personal finance, investing, and wealth building is a path toward empowerment as well. I disagree with the phrase you commonly hear, "knowledge is power." Knowledge isn't power, it's potential power. It only creates power when you do something with it. Knowledge does, however, create confidence. When you have more knowledge about your finances, investing, and knowing how to build wealth, you're able to move forward more confidently.

2. **Direct Your Thoughts**

   If you find you are getting less than desired results in any area of your life, ask yourself, "Are my thoughts about this based on fear?" If they are, then ask, "What do I need to do to shift my mindset to abundance right now?" The sooner you can gather all of the fear-based thoughts you have and rewrite the scripts on each, the faster you'll be on your way to living consistently in that abundance mindset.

3. **Train Your Focus**

   The enemy of abundance is a narrow focus. A Harvard study found that when people focus intently on one thing, other possibilities right in front of them go completely unnoticed (Castrillon, n.d). It's further proof that what you focus on really matters. Opening your mind to focus to what's possible, instead of what's probable, creates the abundance mentality.

4. **Choose Your Words Wisely**

   The language you use, what you tell yourself, what you say about others—all shapes your reality. Are you using language of scarcity or abundance? When you are engaged in conversation, notice what you are saying. When you find yourself talking to someone (or yourself) about something you can't have or aren't able to do (even when it's what you actually want), stop yourself and have the courage to say, "Thank you for listening to me, but I want to take that statement back because that is a scarcity view." Then, say what is possible from an abundance mentality.

5. **Celebrate Daily**

   Make it a point to track daily achievements. Oftentimes we don't see how far we've come or the amount of growth we've already had, so it's important to take time to celebrate the small wins. Just like wealth and investing, your achievements and success compound over time. It's why studies show that the greatest portion of your wealth will be made from age 50 to 60. Your knowledge, your wealth, your life experiences, and the data you accumulate over time, all compound and lead to greater returns.

Broke Belief #2: Future Condition

"Future condition" means how things will be or when things change in the future.

> *This is often an "if" or "when" scenario.*
> *WHEN I have more money, I'll start investing.*
> *IF I make more money, I'll save for my emergency fund.*
> *WHEN I have a better job, I'll start a retirement account.*
> *IF I knew more people, I could start a business.*
> *WHEN I have more time, I'll learn more about building wealth.*

When you feel like you don't have much money, or much extra to begin with, investing may seem pointless. But starting anyways, and starting small, can add up to something truly worthwhile. Consider that few millionaires (at least none that I know) begin their investing careers with huge amounts of money. Most people grow their wealth over a period of years at a (usually) slow but steady pace. By beginning slowly and using small amounts of cash, you can instill the habit of steady, regular investing. This is a consistent habit which will hopefully establish a large nest egg for your future.

The problem with waiting for something else to happen, some future condition, well, there are a lot of problems with it. But the bottom line is all of the reasons you can't begin now are merely an excuse. You don't need more money, a better job, or a different type of investment market to start investing *now*.

Investing is like going to the gym. You have to pick up that first five-pound weight if you ever want to pick up the 50-pound weight. You have to run the first mile if you want to run a marathon. Investing is the same. Start small, stay consistent, and develop the habit.

If you want to provide income for your future—5, 10, or 40 years from now—then *now* is a good time to start investing. Resist the urge of waiting, or looking for a pullback in the markets or particular stock when your goal is long-term financial growth. Waiting to time a market can actually cost you far more because long-term investing is a long-term game. Consider this: The 10% difference on your purchase price today won't matter much in 20, 30, or 40 years when your original investment has grown tenfold!

And the secret to starting small with investing is this: Even if it goes down in the short term, investing is all about the long game. Staying focused and riding out any market dips is the secret to producing long-term gains.

The only caveat to this is if you currently have the Big D—and no, get your mind out of the gutter—the Big D is **Debt**.

The Rule of 7

What do you think keeps most Americans up at night? Is it an uncomfortable bed, a big meal too close to bedtime, or the latest horror flick? Nope, it's actually *debt*.

According to the American Psychological Association, two-thirds of Americans consider that money (or the lack of it) is a major source of stress for them. Because this kind of stress is so common, it has been given a name: *debt stress syndrome.*

Some statistics from the Federal Reserve Bank of New York show that US household debt exceeded $14.56 trillion in the fourth quarter of 2020. This figure is $414 billion *more* than debt reported from the same period in 2019.

Other 2020 statistics, this time from the credit-monitoring service Experian, show average US debt per household to be at $92,727, which is a 10-year high.

The Big D is not only stressful, but also can cause panic and chronic anxiety and lead to poor decision making—which all can be a living nightmare for those who are swimming in it.

Consider that not all debt should be as stressful. Some debt may merit the worry it causes, but other kinds of debt can assist you with setting up a financially secure future. Debt on real assets—businesses, rental properties—can lead to more cash flow and greater net worth, and could fall into the good-debt category.

Think of it this way: If a particular debt *increases* your net worth or has future value, it's good debt. But if the debt simply gives you another payment to make and you're left with something of *less* value than when you purchased it, it's bad debt.

Recognizing good versus bad debt is easy. Does an item lose value the moment you purchase it? If so, that's bad debt. It's true that many of life's basic purchases, such as clothes and cars, fall into this category. But do you really need that 85-inch smart TV to watch football? Do you really need overpriced shoes to wear to that event? Especially when it's the exact thing that's robbing you from creating wealth? Oftentimes, people spend a lot of money trying to "look rich" and "feel rich", but that behavior is exactly what's keeping them from ever *being* wealthy.

Here's a good rule to follow for depreciating purchases: If you can't pay cash for it, don't buy it.

Bad debt is any loan, payment, or interest being paid on depreciating assets—credit cards, paycheck loans, cars, boats, or motorcycles.

And as if that's not enough on its own, the amount of debt you have is always monitored against your income. Meaning, if you want to buy a house, or an investment property, your ability to get funding will depend on the amount of debt you have.

Take a moment to figure your debt-to-income ratio. For example, suppose that you earn $4,000 a month and have these regular debts to cover: a $1,300 monthly mortgage, $400 car payment, and $700 for monthly credit cards and other bills. Your monthly debt is $2400, making your debt-to-income ratio 60%.

A debt-to-income ratio over 43% is a red flag for potential lenders who know that borrowers with a higher ratio are more likely to have issues with making monthly payments. Depending on your lender and other variables, you may not even be able to get a mortgage or secure funds if your ratio is above 43%.

If you have any amount of bad debt, you want to eliminate that *before* you start investing because **there is no greater destroyer of your wealth than bad debt.** That brings us to the Rule of 7.

The Rule of 7 is any debt that has an interest rate of greater than 7% needs to be paid before you start investing.

Historically, the average investment in an index fund such as the S&P 500 that tracks the market will yield average returns of 8 to 10% annually. Obviously there were some years when it was much higher and others when it was much lower, but 8 to 10% has been a consistent average over decades.

The Rule of 7 (RO7) uses this data to support that any debt over 7% needs to be paid before investing and any debt that is good debt that increases your net worth or debt with interest below 7% (mortgages, home equity loans, school loans, etc.) will make more in your investments over time than you'll save by paying down the debt on assets.

So using the RO7, what debt (if any) do you currently have that need to be paid off before you start investing? List them below with the highest interest rate to the lowest:

Name of creditor:	Amount owed:	Interest rate:

Once listed, add your balance and the current interest rate you are paying on each in order of highest interest rate to lowest. Start at the top and begin paying down the Big D. There is no greater enemy to building wealth than debt. Make sure you don't skip over this step before moving forward. Remember, it's not just what you *think*—or even read—that builds wealth, it's what you *do*.

Broke Belief #3: Lack of Appreciation

Often, we feel unappreciated because someone doesn't say the words. Whether it's your efforts at work, the attention you give in a relationship, or taking care of someone in your family—we can feel unappreciated when not acknowledged. Not hearing or feeling appreciated can then lead to resentment. Being in a state of resentment isn't just unhealthy, it blocks you from what you do want. So imagine being given the life you do have and still not appreciating it.

You may not have everything you want, but the fact is you already have far more than a lot of people in the world. Many people around the world live on less than $1 per day. More than **half** of the world population lives with less than $10 a day. So if you bought this book, you are already doing better than half of the people in the entire world. And although you may think for a moment that you have a lot to be grateful for, fixing a *belief* will take more than thinking something once. It will take consistency to change and rewire your focus.

The opposite of a lack of appreciation is gratitude.

Gratitude is beyond something we think about when we are given a gift or when someone does a favor. Gratitude is a practice until it becomes a way of life.

Before jumping out of bed or grabbing your phone to check your email, take two minutes to think about all of the things you're grateful for—a roof over your head, a free country to live in, food in your refrigerator, a job to go to, a family that's healthy—the list is endless.

I wake up every single day deeply grateful to see the sun shining, for air in my lungs, for a heart that beats without any of my own effort—the list is endless. You may wake up and be grateful for the sounds of your kids, a job you worked really hard for, a position/education you busted your butt to get, the clean water you drink, or the income you have.

When you focus on being in a state of gratitude, scarcity leaves and abundance is all around. And I promise you—the more grateful you are, the more abundance you focus on, the more blessings that come into your life.

I'm going to mention this a couple times in the book because it's worth saying more than once. Practicing gratitude is one of the most powerful and widely recognized tools for creating abundance and happiness. There are numerous studies on the power of gratitude for health and overall well-being—not just financially but emotionally, mentally, and physically as well (Stinson, 2019).

Take a moment and start this practice right now. If you choose to, what can you be grateful for right now?

Broke Belief #4: Being Around the Wrong People

This isn't so much a belief as it is an action, but there is an underlying belief in it.

You may think your friends or your family aren't connected to your debt, your spending habits, or your beliefs about money—but unfortunately that's just not the case. Shopping sprees, lavish vacations, sporting events, fancy dinners—and sometimes you have to choose between hanging out with friends and paying the rent.

Your friends aren't necessarily evil, and they may not be trying to sabotage your budget or your financial goals on purpose, but financial peer pressure is real, and it's subtle. And with a world filled with people pleasers, or at least those who don't want to create conflict, it's human nature to want to fit in or go with the flow.

Maybe it's that luxury resort everyone wants to travel to, that new bag everyone starts carrying, the newest iPhone model, or the car you thought was totally fine but now all of your friends have upgraded to a new car while you're still chilling with your 2012 Nissan—and you start to feel a little lack. As your friends talk about the improved back-up cameras, Bluetooth capabilities, and interior cabin upgrades, you feel out of the loop, and maybe a little inferior—so you throw your budget and investment goals to the wind and buy something new (even though your car was working just fine).

It can be hard to maintain a relationship among friends with more money, less discipline, looser spending, or those with no financial or investing goals— because either their expensive taste or overspending is sending you further into debt just trying to keep up (or not be jealous).

So what do you do to stay on top of your goals and not let a friend sabotage your dreams of financial freedom?

Be honest.

Nothing ruins a friendship faster than lying or being fake. If you can't afford to go to the Super Bowl, attend that bougie party, or go on a shopping trip to Neimans, say so. Don't make up a story about why you can't go, be

honest that you are working toward some financial goals and you're going to
sit this one out. Thank them for the invite and for thinking of you, that's it. It
may seem like a big deal, but it's not. And if they are a true friend, they will be
understanding and supportive of you—plus they will have so much respect for
your discipline (that you may even influence them to do the same).

If anyone were to respond negatively to that, trust me when I say—you
probably don't want them having a front row seat in your life anyway.

And remember, you can always make an alternate suggestion on how to
spend time together. Indulge in a good movie on Netflix, go volunteer at your
local rescue, or go for a hike or hit a spin class. Some of the best times I've
spent with friends didn't involve spending a lot of money. You might even find
that avoiding the hot nightclub, Sunday's game, or that party actually gives
you the ability to spend more time together.

One thing no amount of money can buy is great memories.

Friendship should be centered on shared interests and affection, not
competition and who can spend the most. Don't let money get in the way of
friendships. And if you find it still does, even with the above suggestions in
mind, it might be time to find a new friend.

Time for a Wealth Habit Quiz

Do you have any of these thoughts?
Check [yes *or* no] to each statement:

1.	I'll invest when I have more money.	[ ] yes [ ] no
2.	Money doesn't solve problems.	[ ] yes [ ] no
3.	Money is evil.	[ ] yes [ ] no
4.	It's hard to be wealthy.	[ ] yes [ ] no
5.	I don't understand how to invest, so I don't want to try.	[ ] yes [ ] no
6.	You have to be lucky to be wealthy.	[ ] yes [ ] no
7.	I don't have enough experience.	[ ] yes [ ] no
8.	I am not connected enough to be wealthy.	[ ] yes [ ] no
9.	I am just not good with money.	[ ] yes [ ] no
10.	God doesn't want us to have wealth.	[ ] yes [ ] no
11.	I can't do this alone. I need a spouse to have money.	[ ] yes [ ] no
12.	I have so much debt, I'll never be wealthy.	[ ] yes [ ] no
13.	I'm too old to start building wealth now.	[ ] yes [ ] no

14.	Someone else handles this for me; I don't need to understand it.	[ ] yes [ ] no
15.	I'll marry someone rich and won't need to worry about this.	[ ] yes [ ] no
16.	No one in my family has money, we just aren't good with it.	[ ] yes [ ] no
17.	When X happens, then I can fix my finances.	[ ] yes [ ] no
18.	When I get a better job, I'll have more money.	[ ] yes [ ] no
19.	It's too late for me to learn all of this stuff and turn my life around.	[ ] yes [ ] no
20.	Once I have X amount of money, I'll have enough.	[ ] yes [ ] no
21.	People who have money are greedy and selfish.	[ ] yes [ ] no
22.	I feel bad for having more money when there are so many other people in the world who don't have what I do.	[ ] yes [ ] no
23.	My money is going to run out, this is not going to last.	[ ] yes [ ] no
24.	I don't deserve to be wealthy.	[ ] yes [ ] no
25.	No one will like me if I have money.	[ ] yes [ ] no

Let's find out what your answers mean. How many of these statements did you say yes to?

RESULTS

0–5: Money Magnet

You are a money magnet. You are doing great! You have far more positive money beliefs than limiting ones. Earning money, talking about money, and viewing money in a positive light comes to you effortlessly. You enjoy it, you know you deserve it, and you have shaped your views about it. You clearly have the foundation built; now what's important is for us to expand on it. It's clear you've been working on having an abundance mindset and focused your view about money and wealth building with practical solutions. You are ready to start applying the wealth habits and are prepared to take the actionable strategies from the chapters ahead and apply them to your life today! Congrats!

5–15: Money Chaser

You're doing well! You may still be struggling with a few financial blocks, but it looks as if you have done some work on your beliefs about money and overall are ready to start taking the actionable steps to take your belief to the next level. Take a moment and look at the statements you answered yes to. Can you find any similarities that tell you more about where you may be holding onto financial blocks? Where did those beliefs come from? Do you have anxiety around money? Do you avoid talking about your finances? Or maybe you keep giving in to the immediate gratification of buying that new item. Next to where you checked yes, write down where you think that money belief came from and identify how you are going to change it. Once you make adjustments and break through these last remaining blocks, we can start implementing the wealth habits and get you on the road to creating generational wealth. Get ready to become a money magnet.

15+: Money Resistant

If you answered yes to most of these questions, don't sweat it. You are right where you need to be. This is the perfect place and the perfect book to start addressing this resistance head on. It's time to disengage from your negative beliefs and views about money, and now you're one step closer to doing just that.

Your first step forward is to look at each of the statements you answered yes to. Identify where those BS beliefs come from and write it down next to the checkbox. Understand that those beliefs are not true, none of them. It doesn't matter where you heard them, who believed them, or how long you've thought that—they simply aren't true. So flip the script. Write down what is true and start reciting those every day. It's time to change those broke beliefs and start the journey to creating the financial freedom you deserve.

Now, step two, regardless of what your quiz result was, take a look at the questions you answered yes to, and ask yourself how you can flip the script and simply choose a better thought.

Write your answer right next to the statement so when that BS pops up again, you can switch that thought with one that will help you acquire the wealth you deserve.

Your ability to build wealth will depend on your ability to break through these core beliefs. Turning your dreams into reality starts with breaking the habits you currently have and transforming them into *wealth habits*. Only then can you achieve financial freedom. Are you ready for it?

NOTES:

_____

_____

_____

_____

CHAPTER 3

Seven Core Commitments to Make to Yourself

Aside from all the things you need to apply and do in this book, there are a few things we need to make sure you've got straight in your head; otherwise, these will derail you.

There are seven core commitments you must shift toward as you live the wealth habits:

1. Build your belief
2. Be persistent—persistence pays
3. Be solution-focused
4. BYOC—Be your own champion
5. Create your blueprint
6. Be a swift decision maker
7. Start anyway

Build Your Belief

No, this isn't about believing in unicorns and closing your eyes to pretend life is all sunshine and puppy dogs. This is simply having belief—some faith—in yourself.

Because regardless of where you are right now—whether you're tens of thousands of dollars in debt or only have a couple hundred bucks in your bank account—you're going to need to believe in yourself. And if you don't believe in yourself just yet, I want you to lean on *my* belief in you because I know for a damn fact that if I could figure this out and find my way to financial freedom, I sure as hell know you can too.

Moving toward wealth and away from the habits that made you, or are keeping you, broke is going to require you to adopt another set of beliefs. It requires you to have a greater belief in yourself. After all, those other thoughts and patterns you've tried haven't made you wealthy—how about you give this a shot? Are you willing? I'm going to assume you said yes, so let's keep going.

Have the belief you're going to be able to figure out what you don't know. Because there is going to come a time, no matter where you are on the journey, that you are going to feel completely lost. You may feel like an impostor or that you have no idea what you're doing. You may feel you're not worthy, not capable. There may even be a time you think you're not educated enough, connected enough, smart enough. It's so easy for me to say all of the things you may be thinking because I have felt all of them before.

> **There isn't one key to success, but there is one surefire way to failure— listening to the opinions of others and doubting the belief you have in yourself.**

But even in the moments of those fears, those insecurities, those doubts—come back to the wealth habit mindset, come back to the core belief in your gut that you will figure it out and that you *will* get to where it is you want to go. *Belief* is truly the first core principle of what it's going to take for you to get to your next level. This first commitment—to build belief—really compounds over the other six.

Be Persistent—Persistence Pays

This commitment is the one that separates those who achieve their goals and dreams from those who just desire them. Having relentless persistence toward whatever it is you desire most—a successful business, financial independence, a fulfilling relationship—isn't just *important*, it's *critical* to your success. Embracing this habit will carry you through and keep you committed even when it's hard, even when it's ugly, even when people question your ability, question your integrity, even question your intentions.

Because if you haven't experienced that yet, you will.

The bigger you dream, the more that you do, the more you are not only going to be met with resistance but you are going to get taxed, my friend.

It's a hidden tax that doesn't show up on your 1040 or your 1120S, but all wealthy and successful people pay it. It's called the SAW tax. That's right. You've never heard of it, but I bet you've experienced it in one way or another. It's the tax that is reserved for those who are successful, achieving, and wealthy (SAW).

The SAW tax is all the $#%^ you have to deal with from other people when you start achieving success. (Or even just when you start *dreaming* big.)

It's the tax you pay when you achieve big things, have big goals, and dream big dreams. It's when you have that next-level thinking that challenges the status quo, societal norms, or what everybody else in your life is doing.

Why does this tax show up when you *start* becoming successful, achieving, and wealthy? It's not really that people are inherently evil or nasty (although their behavior at times certainly seems like that). But when you go do something big, simply *want* to achieve something more, dream of something different for your life—it will trigger other people.

There are just two reasons why someone would gossip, hate on, or talk about you:

1. **Tangible desire:** They want something you already have—aka envy, which shows up as minimizing, deflecting, gossiping, or judgment. It can even come up as suspicion, doubt, and mistrust. Envy has the ability to snowball into pretty intense emotions and behaviors to the point of being possessive and controlling of that person. And when that doesn't work, they will try and control how others see you.

2. **Intangible desire:** Something about you is triggering the lack in them. It could be something you did or didn't do. It could be something you said or didn't say. You could look like someone they don't like or could have the same name as their bully in school. It could be what they heard about you (from someone else who was triggered by or jealous of you), or it could be because you don't fit the mold of how they perceived you—how they felt you should act, look, or be. It can be your looks, your money, your family, your relationship, your body, your confidence, or your freedom.

> ## It's far easier to talk about someone else than it is to fix yourself.

Why does this happen?

Either consciously or unconsciously they wish they had that big dream, big goal, or that success you're having. They wish they took the chance of going out and believing in themselves and trying for their dreams.

But what those people don't realize is success is here for them too. Anyone can do the work, make the tough choices, take the risks, and go after it all.

Avoid being around or participating in the trap of gossip and trash talk and spend that energy on going out and making the changes you want to make. Remember, no one who is accomplishing more than you will talk about you in a negative manner. Sure they may give you suggestions on that business idea, or that investment you're going to make, or why they may see something different—but they won't gossip about you or try to tear you down for their benefit. **Those who have big goals won't concern themselves with those who have small vision.**

> ## Care more about your dreams than other people's opinions.

When you're met with outside resistance, when the people closest to you (or those you've never even met) toss their hate, shade, or judgment your way, you have two choices:

Quit and let them win, or
Win by continuing to move forward.

If you don't master this one habit, you'll end up spending so much time being mediocre that you'll miss being magnificent.

Be Solution-Focused

I once heard one of my mentors, Tony Robbins, use a great analogy on positive thinking, "You don't just go out into the garden and chant 'there's no weeds, there's no weeds, there's no weeds' while there are weeds all around you."

Solution-focused thinking (or a solution-focused approach) is the understanding that problems happen all the time, but we are going to remain optimistic about the outcome. This does not mean becoming delusional. We know there are weeds, so we find a solution by grabbing gloves and starting to pull them out.

Our brains are wired the opposite way, toward problem-solving. It analyzes the problem thoroughly before generating solutions. Although this route can produce some ideas, it will often lead to a negative outcome. The habit to develop is focusing on finding the solution rather than dwelling on the problem at hand.

You might be thinking, "Well, concentrating on a solution sounds simple"—yet common sense isn't always a common habit. Shifting to solution-focused thinking requires a radical shift in our thinking.

How?

First is to start with the end in mind. I call this REO (no, not REO Speedwagon, although who doesn't love them). It's REO—reverse engineered outcomes.

Unlike conventional ways of dealing with problems, we start and act with the (desired) end result in mind.

Focusing on the solution is a proven way of bringing change to people, teams, and organizations. To do this, there are six steps:

1. **Define:** Clearly define the desired outcome (more wealth, greater health, a weedless garden).
2. **Focus:** Focus on solutions (instead of problems).
3. **View:** Look for strengths (rather than weaknesses).
4. **Refine:** Narrow the focus and home in on what's going well (instead of what's going wrong).
5. **Decide:** Decide on what is the next best path toward the end result.
6. **Take action.**

These six steps make the REO method an extremely positive and practical way of making progress in any goal—including building financial freedom.

Here is REO in action. Southwest Airlines had an expensive problem with their planes. It was taking them 40 costly minutes to refuel *each* airplane. They have lots of planes, so that's lots of minutes.

Getting What You Want Starts with Asking Better Questions

They focused on the problem, by asking, "What's the problem? Why are the planes spending so long on the ground?" They discussed all the reasons the planes spent so much time on the ground to refuel. But because of the way they posed the question, they were unable to find a solution.

When they changed to a more solution-focused question and asked, "How can we get the planes to spend less time on the ground?" the ideas poured out. It finally led to Southwest adopting a new way to refuel that took it down from 40 minutes to 12 minutes! They adopted the pit-stop approach that Formula One racing cars use—the solution-focused thinking shifted everything for them, and it will for you too.

Solution-focused thinking requires you to look at the problem differently. But once learned and adopted as the only way you view a problem, it's addicting because then problems become a fun game to navigate through and learn more.

I love going into a large, challenging project that seems impossible to pull off—that's my favorite. I often hear the 248 ways why something isn't going to work out, or the idea is never going to happen. And what used to make me doubt myself when I was much younger now makes me excited to show a few more people what they can accomplish when they believe they can, are focused on solutions, and are relentlessly persistent.

There is power in that. And there is power in knowing that if something comes up along the way or some big obstacle trips up your original plan making it not go as perfect as you wanted it to, you know that that's okay too.

It's like the time when I started the second location for my nonprofit. I already had almost two decades of business under my belt. I had about 13 years of nonprofit experience at that point as well, so developing a second location—a 62-acre farm sanctuary—seemed like small potatoes at that moment.

Although like clockwork, when I announced where the second location would be, everybody was like, "This is an abandoned cattle farm. It's going to take years to rebuild. You aren't going to be able to pull this off. There is nothing there." Well, unless you count the inches and inches of petrified cow manure on the floors, and more cobwebs than you can count, they weren't wrong.

The building was dilapidated and falling apart. The roof was blown off in certain sections as it hadn't been a working farm for almost a decade at that point.

But my self-believing, relentlessly persistent, and solution-minded brain was like, "Okay, we are closing in May, starting construction in June, and we will be open in time to host a 600-person event in October." That five-month timeline threw everyone over the edge: "Oh my God, that's never going to happen!" And then all the problems were listed—electric, plumbing, roofing, debris—and again, those were all problems, but my mind just saw them as opportunities. Opportunities to grow, to learn, to bring people together, and to find solutions for each. I had the belief it would all work out *and* was persistent in making sure I did everything possible to make it happen.

This is why mindset and mantras are only going to get you so far. The idea of wanting something isn't going to do anything to change your life, your health, or your wealth. It's the implementation and execution of that idea that's going to get you there. You can sit around and have belief, but if you don't do anything with it, you'll be in the exact same place you are now.

Now, did everything work out all perfect and the sanctuary was complete in those five months? Oh, hell no! But every time something happened and we got tripped up, we found another solution. And at the end of it all, if we couldn't have had the event there, which would have resulted in us calling everyone we sold tickets to and telling them, "Hey, we didn't get the barn finished for the event, but don't worry, everything is a go, it's just at this other venue instead," it still would have been great. But here's the thing: I would rather have a huge, challenging goal and miss than to have a small, obtainable goal—and succeed. If you give yourself two years, it'll take two years. But if you give yourself five months and it takes seven months, you just shortened your path by more than 14 months! That's time you can be doing something else.

And just so you know the end of the story, we did finish the sanctuary. And even though all the experts said it would never happen, it didn't take two years. It took just under five months. Now was it absolutely hell to get there? It was, but we did it. We hosted our first event there with 600+ people and started saving animals much sooner than we would have if we had taken much longer.

Here's my question to you:

What is one thing you want to accomplish in the next year?

_____

Now what would you need to do if you decided to accomplish it in the next **30 days?**

_____

_____

_____

_____

BYOC—Be Your Own Champion

Another trap that really trips people up in the pursuit of greater wealth and bigger things is having the belief you need cheerleaders, supporters, and other people to help you champion your dream. I'm likely going to ruffle some feathers here, but stick with me. I will save you a lot of hassle, disappointment, and pain if you hear me out on this—**you don't need anyone else to believe in you, that's your job.**

You may think that to start a business, to go after some dream or big goal you need your family, your friends, your spouse, or the damn PTA to support you only to find that very few, if any, of them, will. And that's not their fault—most people are conditioned to seek sameness, stability—keeping us the same so we don't trigger anyone else. It goes back thousands of years, this ancient brain we have and ancient conditioning passed down for generations.

And had we been born in caveman times it would have served us well. We depended on each other to stay together to live, to eat, and to thrive. Because the alternative was death—but we don't need the whole tribe to go out and gather berries anymore to survive.

The sooner you understand you're the only one who is needed to protect your dream, to champion your cause, to rally around your goal—the less disappointed you'll feel when others aren't supportive and the more empowered you become. Because like my friend Anne once told me, "At the end of the day most people can't remember if they put their own garbage out or not"—so they certainly don't have time to care if your business grand opening went well or if you made a million in crypto this year. They have their own dreams, their own goals, and their own problems.

If you are sitting reading this, or driving listening to this, and you feel like you're so alone and you don't have anybody else supporting you or encouraging you or believing in you, guess what—that's okay. The secret is *you can succeed anyway.*

There are so many times in my life that the people closest to me were also the people who didn't want me to do that next thing. People told me investing in properties across the country wasn't a good idea; others thought it was too much for me to add another location, or start another business, even my well-intended dad thought my real estate investing was too risky and I "shouldn't push my luck." It wasn't until years later, and dozens of flips later, that he stopped saying it. Well-intended people who care about you can often be the same people who say these belief-destroying messages. Remember that it means far less about you and your ability and far more about their own insecurities, beliefs, fears, or conditioning.

The times I went after it anyway, the times I championed my own dreams, the times I was my own cheerleader, the times I was the only one in the room who actually wanted this next thing to happen are the ones I am so grateful for. Because I would rather you go after those dreams and fail than to succeed at staying in the same place.

Don't allow someone else's lack of belief limit your own.

Wouldn't you?

You might be the only person in your family who is going to be a millionaire, the only person who is going to be a business owner, the first in your family to move out of your hometown, own a house, buy a plane—whatever it looks like for you—but the one commonality in all of these things is the fact that you'll be met with resistance.

But the only way to ensure this won't happen is to keep yourself really small and stay the same. Don't change, don't grow, and don't become who you were created to be. Staying right where you are is the only way that you're not going to have to deal with some of the storms.

My friend Rory was speaking at one of my business events. I had just introduced him and walked backstage to talk with my production team. When I heard him share the story of the cow and the buffalo, my ears perked up. I had no idea where he was going with this story—during a business conference, no less—but having cows at the sanctuary I was intrigued. I know firsthand how intuitive and smart animals are—much more than most humans give them credit for. After volunteering in animal rescue for almost two decades, I am still in awe of how kind, loving, and intelligent they are.

Rory is from Colorado and he was sharing how his home state has a unique landscape because they have the Rocky Mountains and the Plains.

It's also one of the only places in the world that has both buffalo and cows. He was talking about adversity in life and business and started to share the difference between the cow and the buffalo.

"Both animals know that the storm is coming, but they handle the storm much differently. When storms come, they almost always brew from the west and they roll out toward the east.

"Cows can sense that a storm is coming from this direction. So a cow will try to run east to get away from the storm.

"Now, the only problem with that is that if you know anything about cows, they're not very fast (super playful but not fast). So the storm catches up with them rather quickly, and the cows continue to try to outrun the storm. But instead of outrunning the storm, they end up staying in the storm longer, which maximizes the amount of pain, time, and frustration they experience.

"Buffalo, on the other hand, are very unique in their approach. Buffalo wait for the storm to cross right over the peak of the mountaintop. And as the storm rolls over the ridge, the buffalo will turn and charge directly into the storm.

"They run *at* the storm, and by running at the storm, they run straight through it—minimizing the amount of pain, time, and frustration they experience from that storm."

Notice how it is the *same* storm. Different experiences, same storm.

Charging at the storm, and not running from it, is the shortest path to get through it. That story applies so well to our lives.

We always have storms, and there will always be storms, but how we handle them is what matters.

Be a buffalo. If you're in the midst of a storm right now, or you know that one is coming, make sure you wait it out, be patient, and charge through that storm, because just on the other side is where greatness lies.

Create Your Blueprint

It's often said that knowledge is power, but actually, knowledge is only *potential* power. Knowledge only becomes actual power if it can be put to use as part of an organized plan.

Many people fail because they think the fortune is in the idea—but the fortune is in the execution of the plan. And if one plan fails, understand that defeat is temporary and only means there was something wrong with your plan—which can be fixed if you keep trying until you get it right.

Thomas Edison was defeated 10,000 times before inventing a successful light bulb. James Dyson failed 5,126 times with his vacuum prototype. Sylvester Stallone was rejected 1,500 times in his desire to produce *Rocky*. Elon Musk blew through his $35 million from the sale of PayPal, and in just two years he was officially broke; now he is the richest man in the world.

Ideas are great, but for them to survive and succeed, they must be activated with a definite plan, put into immediate action, and executed with persistence.

If you don't control your finances, they will control you.

When you're building a house you need a blueprint, a set of plans that tells you how the house will be built and what it will look like at the end. This is just the blueprint for what *you* want and how you want your life to look.

So how do you create your personal blueprint?

First, you have to define what you're after.

Do you want to buy your first investment property, move across the country, start a business, get out of debt, live at the beach, have a million dollar investment portfolio? Make sure you know *what* you want—clearly and vividly.

Don't get tripped up. You don't need to know *how* to do these things, or when you're going to do these things, or if it's probable for you to achieve it — you just have to decide what it is you truly want.

Imagine I have a magic wand and can make your wish come true but only if you can clearly define what it is that you want to achieve. Do you have it yet? Don't move on until you do. Imagine what you want to have, achieve, do, or give.

Okay, now that you have clearly seen it, we need to get it out of your head and onto paper. Life is busy and hectic, and in order for you not to get pulled into the reality of *what is*, I need you to be visually reminded of the reality of *what is to come*.

Visualization is based on actual neuroscience and how the brain works. When vision *and* strategic action is combined, it can seem like magic, but it is just the result of us using more of our brain's potential in a structured, practical system.

1. Clearly define what you want.

2. Take a moment to see it, imagine it—as if it has already happened.

3. Transfer that scene from your mind and create a physical reminder of it. This can be done visually with graphics and pictures, written on paper in words, or combination of both (which studies show are most effective).

4. Set an alarm on your phone and for 2 minutes every day, review that physical reminder.

5. At the end of those 2 minutes, ask yourself this question: "What is my next best step to achieve this?" and write down the answer. Practicing this one exercise daily can change your life.

We know it's possible to turn your dreams into reality. We have proof all around us. But it's not magic. It's simply an idea, put into action and coupled with hard work.

And it's not something that happens overnight. For success in anything, you have to set your intention, believe that it will become a reality, then take active steps towards making that idea come to life.

There is actual science behind how this works. It doesn't work alone, but it helps everything else and is extremely effective. Neuroscientist Dr. Tara Swart explained it by saying, "It primes the brain to grasp opportunities that may have otherwise gone unnoticed. That's because the brain has a process called 'value-tagging,' which imprints important things onto your subconscious and filters out unnecessary information" (Doherty, 2017).

In *Psychology Today*, Dr. Neil Farber pointed to several studies that showed people who visualized a positive outcome were more likely to take concrete steps to make their goals happen.

It isn't by chance that years ago I put a photo of a big white stucco house with a terra cotta roof and a governor's driveway lined with palm trees in the town I wanted to live in—just so happens to be the house I bought a couple years ago (and that's one story of many). It isn't by chance that client after client I work with check goal after goal off their blueprint—financial goals, health goals, family goals.

Steve Harvey, Oprah, Ellen along with numerous pro athletes and Olympians have all shared that creating a visual picture of what they want has helped them create the life they have.

So if you aren't where you want to be just yet, trust the science—and the data—and give it a shot.

Be a Swift Decision Maker

One of the most common mistakes people make and reasons why they fail at ever becoming wealthy is not because of their lack of knowledge or lack of desire, it's their inability to make a decision and stick with it.

Successful people reach decisions quickly and move with speed, not allowing distractions to sidetrack them from their plan.

Unsuccessful people do the opposite: They put off making decisions and, once they've finally decided to do something, they change their minds quickly and focus on something else. This "shiny object" syndrome makes it impossible to move consistently toward a goal, let alone achieve it.

Have a reputation for being decisive—act decisively and stand firm on decisions. Procrastination, the opposite of decisiveness, is a common obstacle you must overcome—not just in your finances but in all areas of life.

People who can't reach decisions promptly and stick with them are easily influenced by the opinions of others. Allowing others to do their thinking for them means they will end up just like the masses—broke.

Decisive people are not bothered by others' criticism—they do what they want, regardless of what others think.

> ## If you want to have success at building wealth, or anything else in life, you must develop the habit of being decisive.

Indecisive people, on the other hand, take others' opinions to heart, weigh out all the options, and end up in analysis paralysis—not moving forward with any type of confidence or speed. This lack of confidence often leads to insecurity.

Start Anyway

Action breeds clarity. And all action begins with a decision to start.

When it comes to the idea of starting even when you've not ready—everyone else balks at the idea or comes up with a good reason for why the time isn't right. But successful people figure out how to take the first step—even if it seems outlandish.

If you want to summarize the habits of successful people into one phrase, it's this: Successful people start before they feel ready.

When I was right out of high school starting my first business, I wasn't prepared.

When I started a nonprofit at 26 years old with no experience or clue how to make it work, I wasn't qualified.

When my publisher gave me a deadline to write the book you're holding right now, I wasn't sure if I could do it.

Of course, you want to put things out in the world that are of quality, with excellence, and for the right reasons—but don't use that as your reason not to start. Seeking perfection is simply an excuse not to try because you fear failure more than you desire success.

If I had gone to college and waited four years to start my first business, I would have missed out on so much—lessons, revenue, impact, friendships, wealth, personal and professional growth.

If I would have waited to start a nonprofit until I was in my 40s, we wouldn't have saved thousands of animals, we wouldn't have helped as many people heal, and we wouldn't have had the impact we've had.

If you're working on something important, something big, something meaningful—you'll never feel ready. You're bound to feel uncertain, unprepared, and unqualified.

> **If you wait until you are fully prepared to do something, you'll wait and never accomplish anything.**

But once we get the BS beliefs out of the way, and you make the decision to increase your financial intelligence, let me assure you of this: What you have right now is enough. You can plan, delay, and revise all you want, but trust me, what you have now is enough to start.

It doesn't matter if you're trying to start a business, lose weight, build wealth, or achieve any number of goals—who you are, what you have, and what you know *right now* is good enough to get going.

We all start in the same place: no money, no resources, no contacts, no experience. The difference is that some people—the winners—choose to start anyway.

No matter where you are right now, start before you feel ready. Rest assured that this book will give you the steps, but building *wealth habits* first starts with your decision. Are you with me? Let's dive in!

WEALTH HABIT 2

Learning Your Way to Wealth

CHAPTER 4

The Compounding Dividends of Self-Education

"Higher education will give you a job and pay you a salary; self-education will give you freedom and pay you a fortune."

My parents were 16 and 19 when they found out they were going to have me. I grew up in a small white trailer on a patch of ground that my grandfather rented to my parents to park the trailer on. Needless to say, they did not go to college. They were too busy working hard just to survive.

My dad had dropped out of school in 9th grade to work at the landfill, and my mom dropped out right after 10th grade to have me. We were on government assistance programs when I was first born. No one on either side of my entire family had ever gone to college—or had any money for that matter.

This is the point in the story where you might expect me to say, "And I ended that tradition by being the first one to go to college!"

No, I didn't go to college. Instead, I pursued a path of *self-education in real-world life and business skills*—a path you can walk as well, whether you've been to college or not.

In my self-education, I learned how to build a business, how to live on less than I earned, how to invest my money, and how to build real wealth—all self-taught, through self-education. You're going to learn these things too in this book.

Most people don't think that a chapter called self-education belongs in a book titled *Wealth Habits*. However, you'll see from my own story (and countless others), self-education was critical to my financial success—and how formal education in college would have actually held me back. I might be stuck in an office cubicle somewhere, drowning in debt to get that piece of expensive paper—aka a college degree.

I am grateful to my parents for their support and for being so flexible when it came to my decision, rather than doing the typical thing parents do. They didn't push me into college—which would have prevented me from working and earning money while I accumulated expensive "credentials"— and the debt to go along with them.

Teenage parents and poverty aside, I had a very atypical upbringing. From first grade through high school, I went to religious school. It bordered on a cult, but it wasn't a full-on cult like you see in Netflix documentaries. It was more like "cult light": if cults were graded like beers, my school would have amounted to Coors Light of cults—most of the taste, half the calories of regular cults. But it was still insanely strict. Lots of control and power.

Girls weren't allowed to wear pants, we weren't allowed to wear shorts. Only "proper" (aka long) skirts and dresses. We weren't allowed to have dances, hold hands with boys, listen to rock music, or go to the movies. The closest thing to shorts or pants were these hideous culottes we had to wear in gym class. I'll save you from googling what those are and tell you that they are an odd, ugly piece of clothing that are shorter than pants, but definitely not shorts. They weren't fashionable, or even sold in stores, so they had to be homemade. Basically, we weren't allowed to do anything teenagers love to do. As a strong-willed, strong-headed teen—who was always pretty self-aware of how messed up that whole situation was—I did everything I could to try to get expelled. But I kept being forced to go back.

I could not wait to get the hell out of there, and I finally graduated with an academic scholarship to Ohio State University. I wanted to get a degree in criminology and be in the FBI. I know that's a hard right turn from where I am and what I do now. Why the FBI? That's a longer story, which I'll share in another book. But let's just put it this way: Like many young girls, I was sexually abused as a child. It took me 20 years to ever talk about it, but looking back I can see why I wanted to be in the FBI. I wanted to do as an adult is what I couldn't do as a little girl—have a voice (and a badge) to hunt down perpetrators that hurt people and put them behind bars so no one else had to experience what I did.

I realized very quickly, however, that to go to college, I was going to have to spend four more years in school (and I was not a fan of school at this point, to put it mildly) and rack up tens of thousands of dollars in debt beyond whatever the scholarship provided—all to get a $30,000 per year entry-level job once I graduated. It just didn't make sense to me.

The summer before I was to attend OSU, I took a couple classes at my local community college to get a better feel for college (secretly hoping I'd like it). I had tested out of some of the basic college classes and recall being in a business class (which seemed like kindergarten to me as I had spent almost my entire life working *in* a business to this point—more on that later). When I asked the professor what businesses he owned, he stated, "I don't own businesses, I work as a professor here." And I remember my 18-year-old self thinking, "If he hasn't ever owned a business, how the hell is he teaching me about one?" And that's when it shifted for me. I was already having trouble making sense of the whole college thing before that day (but getting a scholarship to OSU seemed pretty cool and clouded my judgment for a minute); however, that small exchange in the first week of that class confirmed what I already knew. And it was "peace out" for me. I knew I wanted two things: I didn't want to be poor, and I didn't ever want to depend on anyone for money, ever.

Don't get it twisted. I'm not bashing anyone for choosing to go to college. What I am bashing is the crazy belief that *everyone* should go without question (and without doing a cost analysis first!). I have lots of friends, and clients, who have degrees. Some of them use them for their career and love it, and some of them hire me to get out of those careers!

Even if you have a degree, this chapter, and certainly this book, is for you. Because, like legendary coach Lou Holtz said, "You are either growing or dying." Having a degree in one area could be great, but learning and being a student of many areas is a lifelong journey. Self-education is a constant and never-ending pursuit that will pay dividends in your business, your bank account, and your life.

Because there is a huge difference between higher education and self-education.

What Is This Concept of Self-Education?

Self-education is **the act or process of educating oneself by one's own efforts—through reading and/or informal study.**

Formal education is a structured education and training designed on a set of ideals that govern the curriculum, models, teacher plans, instructor requirements, testing and assessments, and class size. This model runs from elementary school through secondary school and on to college.

Formal education covers the subject matters deemed to provide a level of education and training to receive degrees and certificates that will help verify your achievements.

Self-education is the act of acquiring knowledge or skill without having someone else teach it to you. You seek to learn knowledge yourself without any formal instruction, and you become educated without formal schooling. Simply put, you choose what to learn, at what level, and how much of any particular subject.

A self-educated individual can aim to learn a little bit about everything (generalist), or they can work hard toward mastering a single subject (specialist). Either way, it is the act of taking your own learning into your own hands. Because you control the pace and depth on any topic, there are literally no boundaries on self-education.

> **Higher education focuses on having the answer; self-education focuses on *finding* the answer.**

Self-education can free you from a job you hate or a college major you aren't excited about. You don't need to apply for it, nor do you need to wait for an acceptance letter. All you need is a desire to grow and a belief that if someone else can do it, you can figure it out too. It is desire coupled with belief that will ultimately lead you to personal and financial success.

Nowadays, self-education in any topic has become as easy as firing up a Google search bar and doing some research. You can find courses, books, and trainings focused on tech, communication, business, investing, and even basic life skills. But despite this incredible access to information, few people take full advantage of the opportunity available for self-directed learning.

> **Formal education provides you with prominent certificates; self-education provides you with practical knowledge.**

But let's back up a bit. Like I said, my childhood was not typical. Religious cult school aside, there were some other not-so-common (but good) things too.

When I was about five years old, my dad was fired from his job. He was 24 years old, had $200 to his name, and a family to provide for. He was driving home that day and saw a sign outside the local family-owned auto parts store that read, "For Rent - $400 /month." He walked into the store and talked to Stella, the woman who owned it. He inquired about the sign and explained his situation; then he pulled out the only $200 he had from his pocket and asked, "Is there any way you'd let me work off the rest?" She agreed, so my dad started an auto repair shop in the basement of her building.

From the time I was in kindergarten until I was 16 years old, my school bus driver, Janice, dropped me off at Stella's auto parts store every day after school. I'd step off the bus and walk right into the store. I'd prop myself up on one of the stools they had sitting at the parts counter. I'd chat with Stella and her sons,

Al and Ron, who helped her run the store—get a piece of candy they always had for me—and then I'd walk down to the basement to my dad's garage.

Rather than learning how to play soccer (or something else I'd never use in my adult life), I grew up having to have conversations with customers, typing invoices on the typewriter (does anyone know what those are?), answering the phone, and making appointments—all while doing my math and science homework in the back office.

I remember numerous times overhearing customers saying they felt bad or "sorry for me" that I had to go there every day, but I didn't know anything different. I thought it was fun filling up the pop machine, collecting change from the vending machine, and crushing all the empty soda cans so we could take them in for recycling on the weekends.

In between working and homework, I would watch cartoons on the little 13-inch TV in the office or ride my strawberry shortcake bicycle (with the big banana seat and pink streamers) around the gravel parking lot and in between the cars waiting to be repaired. But what I looked forward to most was getting an after-school snack and a cold can of Pepsi from the vending machines. Sometimes, if I was lucky, it would be so cold, it would have a little ice in it and taste like an ice-cold slushie. I'd open up my Reese's peanut butter cups and plop down on the big chair behind the desk. And then, my favorite part of the day: getting to see my dog, Harley, one Reese's cup for me, and the other one for her (obviously, this was *before* knowing chocolate is bad for dogs).

So it seemed like a natural progression from working in the office and answering phones to learning how to drive a car—when I was seven.

My dad had this little, beat-up blue Mazda. It had a bad bearing on a connecting rod, which caused an engine knock that got louder as I accelerated. Imagine seeing a seven-year-old little girl sitting on pillows in the driver's seat, while hearing this loud—tak tak tak tak—sound as she drove by.

You might be wondering, did I learn how to fix cars? No, definitely not, but I did know my way around. I could pick up on patterns like certain sounds and common issues. Which was funny because I did know more about cars than any guy I ever dated.

And every month of those 11 years, I remember Stella—with her flaming red hair styled to perfection, layered in far too much perfume, decked out with gold jewelry around her neck and a ring on every single finger, driving her fancy Cadillac—coming downstairs to collect my dad's rent.

This was where my real education came from. I learned all the nitty-gritty of running a small business. I know I would not be where I am today had I not received my after-school education inside of a small business.

Even more important than some of the business specifics I learned (such as customer service and office management) was the psychology I learned. I saw how my father managed the ups and downs of the business. I saw how he had to swallow his fears and keep going. I learned about determination and persistence. I learned about the mindset of providing quality service to customers and taking care of people (even when it wasn't convenient for yourself).

When I was 19 and running my own business, I learned about all of that and more—in real time. Meanwhile, my friends were sitting in their college classes, learning about "business" from some professor who never ran a real business in his life. (Here's a lesson they won't teach you in college: Don't take business advice from people who have never built an actual business.)

Many kids my age were about to graduate with tens of thousands of dollars in student loans. They had no idea how to provide value to or work with customers—something I had been doing and learning about, in real life, for years—and were surprised when they had difficulty getting hired.

Surprise! Unless you know how to add value to a business and its customers—who are the lifeblood of that business—you're not really that valuable to a company. The only exception is if you know how to add value to the people in the business who *do* add value to customers (such as being a great administrative assistant). But ultimately, everything comes down to adding value to customers, either directly or indirectly.

Colleges don't teach that—because they don't actually have to fight for customers the way businesses do. (Or actually, I should say, the way "non-college" businesses do, since colleges are large businesses with marketing budgets, even if they're "nonprofit.")

Imagine what would happen to the demand for college degrees if the taxpayer subsidies (that's right, you're paying for kids you don't have to go to colleges you don't support) were revoked, or low-interest loans were not made available to teenagers who otherwise can't even qualify for a $2,000 credit card at 23% APY.

Think about that for a minute. We as a culture give 18-year-olds $100,000 in loans to get a college degree, when in most cases we won't even give them a $10,000 loan to start a business!

I'm not saying those policy shifts should or shouldn't happen. I'm just pointing out that colleges don't face market realities because demand for their services is propped up by taxpayer funding and cheap federally backed loans. (This also allows them to jack prices up, which requires further subsidies for their customers, in a vicious spiral of skyrocketing unaffordability yet resulting in more money for the colleges!)

You shouldn't expect people who face no market discipline whatsoever in their lives—whose entire business model is based on inflated demand due to government policy—to teach you anything useful about actually surviving and thriving once you graduate and are thrown into the harsh reality of market discipline.

Our culture is weird—we let young adults swim in the sheltered kiddie pool until they're 22. And then we throw them to the shark tank of market reality when they graduate. Instead, kids should be eased into the realities of work, responsibilities, and markets over time, as was fortunately the case in my own young life.

Again, I'm not totally against college. If that's all you got out of this chapter—you missed my entire point. You definitely need it for certain things. If being a doctor, a lawyer, an astronaut, or an engineer is your chosen field, then it's a necessity. But aside from certain degrees, I just don't think a formal education is needed by the masses today. And certainly not as much as it once was.

Sure, we all need the fundamentals of education; reading, writing, math, and even general basic knowledge of history, science, and geography.

The earlier levels of education do a good job in teaching these skills. The issue lies with "higher" education. It's failing time and time again, it's costing more and more, and—what's worse—nothing is being done about it.

The general societal belief is that a higher formal education is better. The certificates, the degrees, and the "achievement" will set you on the path to getting a good career and great paycheck.

That belief is the reason why college isn't really questioned and ends up being the next step after graduating high school. Graduate high school, go to college, marry someone, buy a big house with 3.5% down and an FHA loan, buy two new cars with your now double income that results in five years of payments, have a couple kids, and on and on. Everyone buys the BS, and no one questions it—so the rest of society does the same. But here's what no one tells you: This plan will put you in debt, keep you in debt, and, what's worse, will put a choke hold on all of your time, your money, your focus—and ultimately strangle your freedom.

You're now a slave to the game—work to pay bills.

That's a huge part of what's wrong with formal education. You learn all the things that will make you a slave to the game, and none of the things that will allow you to create your *own* game. Even if you achieve amazing grades, that shows nothing of your knowledge or your readiness to be successful, or wealthy. It shows that you can follow a set of instructions. That's the exact purpose of formal education—to teach people how to follow instructions and sit still long enough to work a nine-to-five job.

You're not going to find freedom that way. And 95% of people are not finding wealth that way either.

After working with thousands of entrepreneurs and founders—and those who aspire to be one—I can tell you what everyone wants. Regardless of whether they are making $50K, $500K, or $5M—they want to create wealth. But wealth is actually just a precursor to get what everyone *really* wants— *freedom*. Freedom to do what you want, when you want, with whom you want, as often as you want—that is true freedom. And that freedom can only be bought and paid for through building wealth.

Your freedom isn't secured until you become financially free.

If you are willing to do a few things that most people *won't* do now, you'll be able to do things that most people *can't* do later. Trust me, I did it.

Don't take my word on this whole theory of true freedom requiring financial freedom. Look at Richard Branson, Bill Gates, Steve Jobs, Mark Zuckerberg—what do all have in common? Yes, they are some of the richest men alive, but they also dropped out of college, pursued their vision, and were students of self-education. And those are just a handful of names. Who we don't hear about is the guy who graduated from Harvard with straight A's who now works for some corporation stuck in a nine-to-five with two weeks off a year, gets a 3% match on his retirement and has hundreds of thousands of dollars in school loans that he's paying off until he's 45 years old.

And look, there's nothing wrong with that path, if that's what you want. Just know, it isn't the *only* path you can take.

We are truly fortunate to have a wealth of information at our fingertips. There are so many online resources that it can at times become overwhelming with all the options. Self-education is a perfect tool to take control of your time and decide what information you find beneficial to your life.

Countless people have decided to give up their nine-to-five jobs in the hopes of making money from their passions. I'm not a huge fan of the "Find your passion and make a business out of it," and I go into that in depth in Chapter 8.

But the fact is: You can be massively successful and succeed at business without much of, or any, formal qualification.

How do you approach self-education?

- Read—expand your knowledge by reading quality books;
- Listen—to TED talks, audiobooks, lectures, and podcasts;
- Learn—build your skills by attending specific training programs, seminars, and courses;
- Model—find expert mentors, trainers, or experienced coaches and learn from others.

If you aren't moving forward, you are falling behind. The only way to keep up is by learning something new every day. With so many amazing free online education resources, everyone has the ability to boost their skills and knowledge. So why pay thousands for a formal education when you can educate yourself for a fraction of the cost?

I list 14 specific online and self-education resources, some of which are absolutely free. You can find more information about the apps, courses, and even trainings from top-notch colleges and universities at **www.candyvalentino.com**.

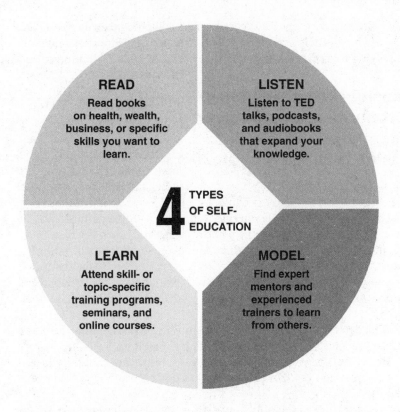

Becoming a millionaire in my 20s, coming from a background with no money, no degree, and no corporate experience, I'm often asked how I learned to do the things I've done over the course of my lifetime. But before I answer that, I want you to know the truth. I wasn't that smart, and I wasn't connected. I didn't do anything unique or even that special. I didn't create some life-changing technology or innovate an industry-shattering product. The "secret" to it all is something everyone can do. The answer is it was hard work and self-education.

Now that I teach entrepreneurship and wealth creation—plus my own experience with it—you may think I would immediately choose self-education as the better education option. But the reality is that both play an important part in our economy.

Our economy is based on ideas, skills, innovation—and taking action on each.

It is not based on certificates and degrees.

"We're in an idea-based economy and a skill-based economy, not a certificate based economy."—James Altucher, self-made millionaire (Elkins, 2017)

One of the mistakes I see most people make is the way they focus on education as a whole. Their expectations, whether for self-education, mentorship, or seeking expert help, is the way they measure their ROI, or return on investment.

> # Remember that our brains can only measure what we lose, they simply cannot measure what we will gain.

Make sure you are learning for the sake of expanding your knowledge and perspective—and not just the sake of making more money. The correlation is there, but don't measure the ROI as not all learning is created equal. You can learn 20 new things (that you'll never use), or I can teach you one thing that will fix a critical issue in your business and will end up saving you from a lawsuit down the road.

The more exposed you are to education, even about fields of no or little interest, the more you can identify opportunities, recognize patterns, and develop your brain to handle a wide range of challenges. It also keeps your neural pathways active in your brain, which is a key factor to keep you healthy.

Learning can even be therapeutic for a troubled mind. It helps discover your unknown potentials, so you stop beating yourself up for failing in one career path. Growing your skill set helps you realize how useful you are to lots of people, and contribution to others makes you happy and mentally healthy.

It's easy to fall for flashing marketing and a well-designed social media page—focus more on who is teaching and the *real-life* experience they have.

> # You do not need to know everything, or be the best at anything to be wealthy. You just have to do a few ordinary things, and over time you will achieve extraordinary results.

So many people don't have access to formal education, but I want you to know this—that will never stop you from being successful.

Gone are the days when formal education was enough to get rich.

Starting a business, increasing your financial literacy, and creating wealth has never been easier, and educating yourself on *how* has never been more available.

The Million-Dollar Argument

The fact that I'm sharing my belief that most young people shouldn't automatically go to college elicits one core argument from the other side—and that is based on the fact that on average college students make more money than non-college graduates.

However, this statistic is used by colleges—and those who advocate for it and *profit* from it. They tend to use it every single chance they get because, frankly, it's one of the only tools they have to counter the argument. And I won't completely disagree as there is truth to it; however, we need to see the entire picture.

On average, people with a college degree in the United States earn about $55,260 a year, while those with a high school diploma earn $40,612.

My friend Michael Ellsberg wrote an entire book called *The Education of Millionaires: Everything You Won't Learn in College About How to Be Successful* on this topic. He explained another way this earnings premium gets regurgitated in the media is on the extrapolated statistic that on average, you'll earn more than a million dollars over the course of your 40-year work life going to college (Ellsberg, 2011).

How do they arrive at that number? They basically take the difference of the two stats, multiply it by 40, which comes out to around a million dollars. But isn't it interesting that this argument is brought forth by colleges, politicians, and lobbyists explaining why you should drop tens of thousands of dollars and go into massive debt to go to college (Ellsberg, 2011)?

What they don't explain or share are the endless number of people who go to college for a certain degree and never end up using it, or those who go and never finish. I have countless friends and acquaintances who went to college for four-, six-, and even eight-year degrees and now work jobs in different fields and don't even utilize their degree anymore. But the colleges and universities fail to disclose this type of information.

In his research, Ellsberg shared that the Arizona State University website (go Sun Devils!) defended a tuition increase stating that "The cost of college education paid through tuition is the best investment that a student can make in his or her future[. . .]. Average annual earnings of individuals with a bachelor's degree are more than 75% higher than those earnings of a high school graduate. These additional sums are more than $1 million over a lifetime (Ellsberg, 2011)."

They literally make it sound like you drop $85,400, which is currently the average cost of a 4-year degree at a public institution, or $150,400 from a private college *after* financial aid and *not* including room and board, and then you'll get a million bucks!

But those who push this narrative have seemed to have forgotten something.

Two little words tied together mean something big: opportunity cost.

One of the Most Important Concepts You'll Ever Learn

Opportunity cost is a central concept in investment analysis. Talking about investments without talking about opportunity cost or without evaluating it in the consideration of this conversation is like trying to determine if your favorite NFL team won the Super Bowl based on *their* score alone—you need to know what the other team's score was in order to find out who won the championship.

Let's use me as an example. Had I gone to college and gotten a criminology degree to be in the FBI, as I had intended, I would have started out with a $37,842 salary back in 2001. Instead, I started my own business in 1999. The first year in my business, I worked my guts out and had a net profit of $3000. The next year, I was only two years in business and I made less than $20,000 that whole year. Seems like college might have been a better decision. But that's because we are only evaluating part of the data.

Had I gone to college to get that $37,842 per year, I would have missed out on my third year in business, when I made twice that salary, and year four, when I made six figures in net income.

Back to our example of college tuition above, if we are going to look at what going to college can provide you with, we have to analyze the other side to see what it can be costing.

What would happen if instead of spending the $85,400 to go to college, you invested it or took a different path?

If you invested the same $85,400 in a passive index fund and held it over the same 40-year period the colleges are promoting on their website and if we go back to the long-term annualized rates and returns of the S&P 500, which has been around 9.3%, let's figure out what the return on that investment would be:

In this analogy, instead of paying $85,400 to $150,400 on tuition—and losing four years of your working life—you would be investing it and start working right out of high school.

We'll use the public tuition average of $85,400, earning 9.3% annualized, over 40 years in a passive index fund, and you'd end up with $3,473,803!

So even if you invested that money and just sat on the beach, traveled the world, or created a YouTube channel, and never added another dollar to that account—you would still have over a million *more* at the end of those 40 years than you would compared to the average earnings of a four-year college degree. Blows your mind, right? But let's take it one step further.

There isn't just a difference in money, there is a difference in time *and lots of it*. If you spend even just four hours a day in class, plus two hours on homework, five days a week, you're basically working a full-time job. If you worked those same amount of hours, even at a minimum-wage job at the country's current average of $9.88—that would give you $395.20 a week or $20,550.40 a year. But we know you're not going to take a minimum-wage job, especially with the job market in 2022, and we haven't even figured out the opportunity if you started out a business like I did right out of high school.

When you look at the facts, investing $85,400, $150,400, or $250,000+ in school *could* be a good decision if someone is looking for a specific profession that they love and will make them happy. But the thought process that kids who graduate *have* to go to college is a joke. And that's not just my opinion. When you look at the numbers, you can see that it's fact.

Of course, I'm not actually suggesting anyone take their college tuition and invest it in an index fund. I'm merely making a point to consider other options for yourself, your kids, or those you talk to about the subject.

Just imagine if you took that time and money and invested it in the kind of real-world education and experiences explained in detail throughout my book. *That's* where the real payoff can be found, and that's when you're on your way to developing the real *wealth habits* needed to start creating true financial freedom.

CHAPTER 5

The Four Crucial Lessons We Didn't Learn in School

In my work with thousands of entrepreneurs, many of whom are millionaires and even billionaires—and who have accomplished many of the things that I know you too are able to accomplish—I have noticed they share four common denominators around beliefs they hold and lessons they've learned.

But these four crucial lessons are never talked about in school. Instead, we're taught geography that we can find on Google Maps. We're taught about algebra and calculus that the vast majority of people will never use again—since the majority of people are not going to become engineers, scientists, or mathematicians. We're taught dates of ancient wars that have nothing to do with us, which we could look up on Wikipedia if we really cared.

In this chapter, we're going to learn these four lessons missing from what is taught in schools. These lessons apply to every single aspect of your life, not just in business or wealth building. They also apply to relationships, being an employee, and just being human in general. Learning these things earlier will keep us from making a lot of mistakes in life. Most of the time people have to go through difficult life experiences to learn these lessons. So if we can understand them and conceptualize them *now*, as opposed to waiting for the hard knocks of life to learn them later, all the better.

There are a few things that college, a formal education, or even a business book will never teach you. So I'm going to change that and put them here in mine. They are:

1. Play the long game;
2. Show up anyway;

3. Nothing is owed to you;
4. Learn the power of gratitude.

Let me break down each.

Lesson 1: Play the Long Game

Today, more than ever, many people are distracted by short-term outcomes.

Everyone is looking for an angle, a hack, a get-rich quick scheme, building their lives on temporary solutions that may appear helpful but are really the newest shiny objects that do not stand the test of time.

Rarely does anyone *seek* to delay gratification. But if you choose to focus on long-term gains and ignore the instant gratification of a short-term win—you can build more than you can ever imagine.

All of life's greatest returns come from compound interest.

Whether you are compounding money, relationships, or skills–time is your greatest force multiplier.

> **Whether it's money, relationships or skills, all of life's great returns come from compound interest because time is your greatest force multiplier.**

And that means you want to play the long game. You want to delay gratification now so you can get *more* later. The process may appear boring or sound challenging, but I promise you—it works. Successful businesses, investors, wealth creators, and entrepreneurs all play the long game to maximize returns.

Here's how:

Invest your money now, instead of spending your money now.

Warren Buffett is worth about $86 billion. The majority of his wealth (99.7% of it) was created *after* his 52nd birthday. This is because of the power of compound interest. The greatest gains are found at the **end** of the compounding period.

There are people who go their entire lives without ever realizing the awesome power of compound interest.

This present moment, the moment you are reading this book, this page, this sentence on this date is connected to the future—through the power of compounding.

Don't allow short-term satisfaction to be more important than the outcome you want for your life.

Do the things that are hard now but good for you later, and your life will get easier and easier over time. That is the definition of playing the long game.

What are you going to give up now for you to get more later?

Yes I'm literally asking you right now. It is eating out far too often? Is it trips to your local shop? Is it the expensive cable TV package? Your ability to give up something in the short term will not only have a direct result on your wealth, but it shows you how much you actually want it.

_____	_____
_____	_____
_____	_____
_____	_____
_____	_____

It is going to take longer than you think (and likely longer than you want)—but if you play the long game when it comes to your life, your business, your wealth, it'll be _more_ than worth it.

The long game applies to more than just compounding capital, it applies to relationships.

The goal is to find and then stick with the people you want to work with for decades. It takes time to build trust and a deep relationship—in business or otherwise.

This becomes difficult if you are constantly switching careers, industries, or moving to new locations. Every time you change paths, you have to start over with a new set of "players." These are people that you don't know, don't trust, and who likely don't trust you either.

I've experienced this firsthand. I moved from Pennsylvania to Arizona in 2019. After building deep friendships, partnerships, and connections for more than two decades in business, it was hard to start over. My network was exceptionally strong, and although there has never been a day I have regretted or questioned the decision to move, I do wish I would have done it sooner.

Most people don't think about where they want to live, where they build their friendships, where to raise their kids. They just keeping living life often times right where they were born. And that might be just fine but know that this decision has a massive impact on the trajectory of your life. Regardless your current age, it's something you want to consider and choose wisely.

Playing the long game simplifies into a sentence—take the necessary steps now to set yourself up for long-term success.

When it comes to building wealth, scaling a business, or creating success in any area of life, playing the long game is a necessary component to hedge the game in your favor.

Lesson 2: Show Up Anyway

Show up when you have no idea what to do, show up when you don't want to, show up when the cameras are off—your commitment to figuring it out, your dedication to be resilient will play a huge role in your success in any area of life.

In fact, a common saying indicates that 80% of success in life comes from just showing up.

It shows how developing the simple habit of showing up can ultimately lead to success. It can also be a powerful part of the puzzle for achieving your goals, building more wealth, and creating a more vibrant, happy, and healthy life.

So, just dive into the concept of "showing up" and its potential positive effect on attaining success.

By committing to consistently show up, you are also committing to the things in your life that matter most. For example, the idea of showing up daily for your financial goals, showing up regularly for your family and friends, or showing up for your personal dreams creates the habit and builds the practice of staying consistent.

The best practice to develop is one that commits to taking even the smallest step forward—because just like investing, those small steps forward compound into larger returns.

Showing up can positively affect your life in these ways:

1. Showing up is **acceptance** in practice.

    When you commit to showing up regardless of challenge or convenience, you put your focus on moving forward with positive action regardless of how small the outcome. Showing up isn't taking large steps every once in a while, it's about doing small things consistently knowing that the results *will* happen. You do the best you can and accept what the timeline may be.

2. Showing up is **dedication** in practice.

    When you dedicate yourself to being there for any area of your life, you handle setbacks, being derailed, or having to pivot. Whatever the circumstances, you continue to follow your goals, make adjustments, and just show up.

Taking even the smallest actions forward can reshape your life. Suppose that you think about cutting your regular gym visit, try showing up and joining in for at least part of the activity. By showing up even when you don't feel like it, you combat procrastination and start building the muscle of resilience—until it becomes an integral piece of who you are and how you are wired.

3. Showing up puts **resilience** into practice.

Your feelings, or excuses, are not facts. Excuses are negative emotions: anger, sadness, guilt, limiting beliefs—all fear-based emotions. These fear-based emotions act as a form of protection, but they actually prevent you from having the very things you want, and deserve.

Letting go of the excuses and showing up even when you don't want to is simple when you become more committed to your *goals* than to that which you *fear*.

At the core of this habit is resilience. Resilience is advancing toward your goals (or that which you desire) despite adversity. It's adapting well and pushing forward even when faced with challenges or stress.

Here are four ways to practice the habit of showing up—even when you have excuses not to:

1. **Be more committed to your *vision* than your *excuses*.**

Get so clear on your vision and desired outcome that you *want* to show up.

Without clarity, we cannot change. It's the very first step to achieving anything in our lives.

Personal clarity is essential to becoming and remaining resilient because without it we waffle in our decision-making and will easily waver in the face of adversity.

Establishing a clear picture of who you are, what you want, and how you plan to achieve your goals is essential. Your vision has to be clear and vivid; otherwise, you will be pulled in different directions that ultimately lead you away from your goals and values.

2. **Build your own emotional stability.**

Be intentional and not reactionary. Having emotional stability—remaining calm and in control of your emotions—will keep you in control of your emotions and not the other way around.

Find ways to regulate your emotions so you aren't easily triggered—meditation, exercise, taking a walk, being in nature—but the number one way to control your emotional state is through what I call "the pause."

Here's how this works in real life. When you find yourself faced with a challenge or adversity, when someone or something triggers you in a way that would typically create an emotional, reactive response, I want to invite you to pause and create emotional stability.

The Pause Reprogram™:

o Pause for one half of one second. A fraction of a second—that's all it takes for our ancient subconscious brain to kick in and blurt out some emotional, reactive response.

o Take three deep breaths without saying a word. Be okay with the silence, and don't try to fill the silence with words or thoughts.

o During those three breaths find one thing you're grateful for—it is impossible for your brain to process pain and gratitude at the same time, so finding one simple thing will lessen your stress response.

o In high-conflict cases, give yourself one hour to fully respond so that your nervous system has time to come down from the heightened emotion.

This one shift in how you respond will build the habit of emotional stability and will give you the focus to continue showing up for yourself.

3. **Mind your physical health.**

Proper nutrition, hydration, and a healthy diet contribute to immune health and energy levels, while overindulging in unhealthy foods or drinks makes you feel less than optimal.

Exercise releases endorphins, which can benefit mental health and lead to a boost in energy and focus. Getting adequate rest is essential for maintaining concentration and energy. And taking time to rest may actually *save time* by promoting increased efficiency. But regulating your sleep is also important because it's tough to be committed to show up for anything consistently if you feel terrible.

It is no coincidence that successful people seem to maintain healthy lifestyles. When you are healthy, you can maximize your focus, approach issues with a clear mind, and have abundant energy. These attributes are vital on your path to success.

4. **Connect with others.**

Here's what *The New Social Worker* magazine has to say, "Isolation is the opposite of what we need to foster resilience. Another key to building resilience is connection with others who can validate, empathize, and understand our feelings and experiences" (Luest, n.d).

Like optimism and gratitude, the happiness boost you get from connection with others is crucial to your health and is a key element to building resilience.

> **Showing up is a small but incredibly powerful action.**

Meeting other people and being around those who are progressing along their journey can help show you the path and its possibilities. Learning of other people's experiences and what they have had to overcome is proof that you can, too.

Even in your relationships, it's always more important to be there for the other person—aka show up—than it is to send gifts or make grand gestures.

Lesson 3: Nothing Is Owed to You

This will likely not be a very popular section, but it needs to be said. Entitlement is running rampant, and what most people don't realize is it's actually robbing people of their dreams and can cost you your fortune.

Entitlement is one of the most harmful traits a leader, or a parent, can instill in another person. Entitlement makes it much more difficult to endure life's challenges and adversities, which results in problem avoidance, passivity, and laziness. It also reinforces the belief and expectation that things come our way without hard work and perseverance.

> **The greatest problem in life is the belief that you shouldn't have any.**

But here's the hard truth. You aren't owed perfect parents or perfect health, financial success, or a life without pain and problems.

Life doesn't owe anyone a job, a career, a house, or an iPhone. And as hard as it is to believe, no one owes you kindness or joy, recognition, or validation. Ouch.

What's tough is we live in a culture that barrages us with images of attractive, successful, and wealthy people. All over social media we see flashy houses and fancy cars, six-pack abs and physical beauty, all while appearing to balance their perfect careers and relationships.

And look, don't get it twisted, there's absolutely nothing wrong with having any or all of these things. Hell, I've worked my ass off for them, and if you follow the principles in this book, you'll be able to do the same.

The problem isn't in the *desire* to have those things, it's the belief that life *owes* them to us.

There is a large portion of adults, children, and teens who feel entitled to having everything they want—so when they fail to get the award, the gift, or title at work (or even just if they do something they don't enjoy), they feel victimized.

But life doesn't owe anyone *anything*. It doesn't owe you happiness, it doesn't owe you success, and it certainly doesn't owe you wealth or love. But here's the plot twist—you have the power to create all of it.

There is massive value in acknowledging and accepting that life owes you nothing, and there is great power in knowing that regardless of anything life has thrown at you, you still can achieve, become, or do anything you want in this life. And don't let *anyone* ever tell you otherwise.

Lesson 4: Learn the Power of Gratitude

Even though life doesn't owe you anything, look at all you've been given.

Having gratitude for everything you have, even when you don't yet have everything you want, is one of the core fundamentals to having success, creating wealth, and designing the life of your dreams.

This isn't fluff, or BS—it's backed over and over again with studies and science.

There are two crucial neurotransmitters—dopamine and serotonin—that are responsible for our emotions. Expressing gratitude releases these neurotransmitters, and right away, they enhance our mood and make us feel good.

As I shared above, the brain cannot process pain and gratitude at the same time, just as it can't feel entitled and grateful simultaneously.

You can help strengthen the feel-good neural pathways by intentionally exercising gratitude every day, thereby activating its long-term effect on the brain.

Gratitude significantly affects body functions and reduces psychological conditions such as stress, anxiety, and depression.

In the brain, the limbic system is in charge of all emotional experiences. You find five parts in this system, including the thalamus, hypothalamus, amygdala, hippocampus, and cingulate gyrus.

Also, the two main sites that regulate emotion, memory, and bodily functions are the hippocampus and amygdala. In studies, these sites are shown to be activated by feelings of gratitude.

Taking it one step further, in a study of individuals looking for mental health guidance, a control group was asked to write letters of gratitude as part of their treatment. This group experienced better feelings, a quicker recovery, and fewer symptoms of death anxiety.

A second group of participants in this study was instructed to journal their negative experiences (instead of focusing on gratitude) along with their treatment. This group reported heightened feelings of anxiety and depression.

After examining the results, it showed that with a grateful attitude in life, we gain acceptance and become fearless of the future.

Gratitude has effects at two levels. At a neurobiological level, it helps regulate the sympathetic nervous system, which is responsible for anxiety responses. At a psychological level, gratitude trains the brain to bypass negative thoughts and concentrate on the positive.

Gratitude practices such as journaling and group discussions demonstrate an influence for reducing anxiety. They are now meaningful mental health treatment tools and are used in interventions and for treating conditions such as PTSD, social phobia, death anxiety, and depression.

Hopefully I don't have to say much more about it, and you can clearly see the massive benefits to being grateful.

Let's be real—if you aren't first grateful for the $5,000 paycheck, you are on a slippery slope, my friend. Because when that paycheck becomes $50,000, you'll be wishing it was $100,000; when it's $100,000, you'll be wanting it to be $1,000,000.

The most common mistake people make on this one is not appreciating where they are, *while* they are on their way to getting what they want. It inevitably keeps you stuck right where you are because if you focus on what you don't have, you'll never have enough. But if you focus on what you *do* have, and are grateful for it, you will end up having more.

Your brain cannot process pain and gratitude at the same time.

Use the *gratitude grid* to begin your practice of being grateful for what we do have. This wealth habit when practiced consistently helps you unlock the next level of life. And yes, there is actually science behind it. Being grateful reframes your focus. Gratitude boosts your neurotransmitter serotonin and activates the brain stem to produce dopamine. Dopamine is our brain's pleasure chemical. The more we think about what we do have with positive, happy thoughts, we feel healthier and happier.

My exercise is: *Before my feet hit the floor, find five things I'm grateful for.*

The importance is you do this even when you don't feel like it. This will drastically shift not just your current focus, but it will change the entire course of your day.

Some examples to get your started:

- Having fresh food to eat;
- The restaurant worker who cooked for you;
- Your health;
- The safe place you live in;
- Having access to clean water;
- The person who cleans your house;
- Your assistant for easing your workload;
- Yourself because you made it out of that situation;
- Clean sheets, warm blankets, the bed you have.

> **It is not happiness and success that will bring us more gratitude. It is gratitude that will bring us more happiness and success.**

Let's get started today. Those who execute and start now will be the ones who win. Take 60 seconds and list five things for today. Use the Gratitude Grid on the next page to get you started right now.

GRATITUDE GRID

MONDAY

1	
2	
3	
4	
5	

TUESDAY

1	
2	
3	
4	
5	

WEDNESDAY

1	
2	
3	
4	
5	

THURSDAY

1	
2	
3	
4	
5	

FRIDAY

1	
2	
3	
4	
5	

SATURDAY

1	
2	
3	
4	
5	

SUNDAY

1	
2	
3	
4	
5	

WEALTH HABIT 3

Earning Your Way to Wealth

CHAPTER 6

The Secrets to Building Multiple Streams of Income

You want your wealth to be flowing like a big river. But do you know how a river gets really big?

By combining with multiple other rivers!

The Amazon River has over a thousand feeder rivers—and each of those rivers have countless other streams.

So let's get set up like the Amazon River (not to mention **Amazon.com**) and get multiple streams of income to contribute to your river of wealth.

Did you know that the average millionaire has at least *four* streams of income?

I know what you're thinking: "What does this actually mean for *me*, and how do I do it?"

I hear you. There is nothing worse than concepts without practical steps to implement. This is why I'm going to break this down in a few easy-to-understand, digestible, actionable chunks.

Investing in real estate—and investing in general—is crucial because you're not just living on the wages from the job you have, or the earnings you're receiving from your business, you're diversifying through other investments and making sure you have multiple sources of income.

That means even when you pull in a good income from your full-time job or business, it is not a bad idea—in fact it's a great idea—to still have additional income on the side. Produce a product, sell a product, provide services, sell on eBay—the more "jobs"—aka sources of incomes you have—the more security you create.

Diversifying your income and having multiple streams is one of the most important things you can do to build wealth.

If a recession, an economic downturn, or a negative financial event hits, and you lose your main source of income, you will have another one, or two, to fall back on as well as assets for a little more security.

There are three ways to earn multiple streams of income, which can be categorized as earned income, passive income, or portfolio income. Let's break down each.

Earned Income

Earned income is income earned from wages, salaries, tips, and other taxable employee compensation—your job, part-time gig, side hustle, and/or your business.

This also includes net earnings from self-employment.

For tax purposes, earned income is any income you receive for work you have done, for either an employer or a business of your own. Regardless of whether your earnings come from a full-time job or a business you own, this money—known as earned income—is subject to higher tax rates than other forms of income you may have. And so, you should use your earned income as funds for investing; it's a practice which will in turn build wealth. Specifically, to take advantage of lower tax rates, move your earned income funds into passive or portfolio income streams.

Wealth Habit : Invest earned income funds → to produce passive or portfolio income

Of course, you can always find other ways to minimize your tax burden. For example, you might take the income through an S corporation, invest money back into your business, or create expenses that are tax deductible. The problem with this strategy is that you have to *spend* in order to save.

You need to be able to earn to save, save to invest, and invest to spend.

Whether you have a day job or own your business, establishing and securing a primary monthly earned income that will support your expenses and allow you to invest is critical to you pursuing these next steps. (I talk more about taxes in Chapter 12.)

Passive Income

Passive income is earnings from a source other than an employer or contractor such as rents, royalties, and stakes in limited partnerships.

In my super simple break-it-down-Candy-like fashion, passive income is something you do once, have little to minimal effort to maintain, yet still receive money for it.

The IRS's definition is: "passive income can come from two sources: rental property or a business in which one does not actively participate."

Because of the depreciation and amortization associated with real estate rental income, such income incurs a much lower effective tax rate.

Suppose that your rental property brings in $120,000 before you deduct for depreciation and amortization. You find that these deductions come to $90,000, and the difference becomes your net taxable income of $30,000.

You're not finished calculating yet. Suppose that your total income puts you in the 37% tax bracket, which means that your tax burden for this net taxable income is $11,100. Now compare the $11,100 in tax with the $120,000 income you received. The effective tax rate you pay on the $120,000 total is 9.25%.

Bringing in that same $120,000 as earned income would require that you spend money (add expenses) to reduce the total income to be taxed. If you don't add expenses and stay in the same tax bracket, you pay 37% of your $120,000—that's $44,400.

When you own rental real estate, you don't actually pay anything for depreciation each year, but you can claim the deduction anyway. That's called a *phantom expense*, and it explains why passive income gives you a tax advantage over earned income.

Passive income is not:

- Your job. Generally, passive income is not income from the wages you earn from a job.
- Your second job. Another job isn't passive income if you'll still need to show up and/or do work to get paid. Passive income is about creating

a consistent stream of income without you having to do a lot of work to get it.

- Non-income producing assets. Investing can be a great way to generate passive income, but only if the assets you own pay dividends or interest. Non-dividend paying stocks or assets such as crypto won't earn you passive income.

Passive income ideas include:

- Rental income;
- Income from an app you create;
- Rent out equipment;
- A bond ladder;
- Affiliate marketing;
- Flip retail products;
- Sell photography online;
- Sponsored posts on social media;
- Rent out your home short-term;
- Advertise on your car;
- Training programs, online courses, or e-books;
- Book royalties;
- Blog or YouTube channel;
- Sell designs or print on demand online.

The goal is to diversify your income streams similar to the way you would your investments.

Now there is a third type of income—and one that commonly gets mixed up with passive income.

Passive income involves some type of money-generating activity you've set up yourself—such as an Internet marketing funnel that "makes money while you sleep" or a long-term rental property that needs little to no management.

Portfolio income simply involves buying an asset that pays you dividends or interest without you having to set anything up (other than buying the asset in the first place).

Portfolio Income

Let's look at the difference and see what assets you can buy to turn your earned income into portfolio income.

Simply put, portfolio income is money received from investments, dividends, interest, and capital gains.

Let me briefly go through **14 examples of portfolio income**.

A **certificate of deposit (CD)** is a savings device with specific characteristics. For example, the certificate has a fixed maturity date and a set interest rate. Also, many CDs specify minimum amounts for the investment as well as holding requirements.

Savings accounts and **high-yield savings accounts (HYSA)** are similar to CDs in some ways, but they do not require a minimum holding period.

US savings bonds are savings products issued and backed by the US government credit standing. They are a low-risk investment and pay interest for up to 30 years.

Money market accounts, also a savings product, consist of high-quality investment securities with a very short term.

Corporate bonds are a savings product issued by for-profit companies. Investors buy these, in essence, to loan money to the company.

Peer-to-peer (P2P) lending happens when individuals obtain loans directly from other individuals without the aid or interference of traditional financial institutions.

Preferred stocks are investments that combine characteristics of bonds and common stock. These are known as hybrid securities.

Dividend-paying common stocks offer dividends to the investors who buy them. In addition, they give investors partial ownership in the company that issues them.

Open-end mutual funds, closed-end mutual funds, and **various exchange-traded funds** are all based on a group of securities. Each type of fund has its own characteristics, but all offer investors diversified collections across single or multiple asset classes.

Real estate investment trusts (REITs) are companies associated with income-producing real estate. A REIT company may own, finance, or manage the real estate.

Master limited partnerships (MLPs) are publicly traded limited partnerships. These businesses (like REITs) can issue common stock and pay dividends.

Ways to Increase Portfolio Income

There are numerous ways you can invest to create portfolio income, but here are **13 ideas** on how to generate additional cash flow.

If you are new to investing, and just getting started on your personal finance journey, I want you to focus on the first one and the last one.

1. **Invest new capital into your portfolio.** Create extra *earned* income over and above your current income. Add that extra money to your investments.

2. **Opt for investments with higher interest rates or yields.** Invest money in the assets with higher rates of returns (ROR). You will create more income from higher rates and yields (which, keep in mind, does take on more risk).

3. **Invest in dividend growth stocks.** Dividend growth stocks are blue-chip stocks of companies that increase their dividend payments regularly. This is one of the most passive ways to increase portfolio income.

4. **Reinvest dividends and interest back into your income portfolio.** Ideally you do not need the income from interest and dividends right now, so you reinvest it back into your portfolio.

5. **Change your mix of portfolio income holdings.** Sell lower-yielding assets from your portfolio. Then, invest the proceeds in some of the higher-yielding examples of portfolio income assets.

6. **Strategically sell holdings in the portfolio.** Our definition of portfolio income includes capital gains. Create income from selling growth assets in the portfolio periodically.

7. **Reduce income taxes on portfolio income.** First of all, reducing taxes depends on your tax situation, but every dollar of tax you save increases the after-tax portfolio income you keep for yourself. It is important to know that some forms of portfolio income receive preferential tax treatment. Specifically, dividends and long-term capital gains. They are taxed at lower rates than interest from savings products. And putting income investments in an IRA can also offer big advantages for investors.

8. **Invest in qualified accounts.** Investing in qualified accounts is another way to reduce taxes. In the US, qualified accounts include the 401(k), 403(b), Roth IRA, and traditional IRA. Depending on the type of account, taxes are either deferred or eliminated.

9. **Keep portfolio turnover low.** Portfolio turnover means how often you buy and sell your portfolio income assets. A certain amount of selling may be necessary for rebalancing or realizing capital gains for income. But do not buy and sell too often as you are more likely to increase taxes and increase transaction costs. The more taxes and transaction costs you incur, the less portfolio income that remains for you.

10. **Reduce investment fees.** Investment fees are another area that can take a bite out of your portfolio income. Mutual fund fees are taken off the top of any income that the mutual fund produces, which reduces the money in your pocket.

11. **Never overpay for investments.** The income you make is inversely related to the price you may pay. Higher prices mean less portfolio income. Look for value, and avoid buying overvalued stocks.

12. **Diversify portfolio income sources.** One of the reasons I provided so many examples of portfolio income-generating assets is for **diversification**. You want to be careful about having all your income coming from just one or two sources.

13. **Invest in low-cost exchange-traded funds (ETFs).** Use a discount brokerage firm for your transactions, and know that many online stock trading platforms are commission-free.

Recently, ETFs are being talked about more. And it is a great tool for those who are newer to building wealth and need a great place to start. So let's break it down before we move on.

An exchange-traded fund is traded similarly to a regular stock; it is purchased or sold on a stock exchange. But this type of security also tracks an index, a sector, a commodity, or another asset. ETF share prices may fluctuate all day, as the ETF is bought and sold. Conversely, a mutual fund trades only once per day, after the market closes. ETFs, which offer US holdings or international holdings, can contain all types of investments, such as stocks, commodities, and bonds.

An ETF may track individual items such as the price of a single commodity or represent a group of securities that are many and varied. For example, the SPDR S&P 500 (SPY) tracks the S&P 500 index.

Investing in ETFs is easier than ever, and choosing this type of fund for your investments (rather than buying individual stocks) comes with lower expense ratios and fewer broker commissions.

Before jumping right on the EFT bandwagon, consider putting in these efforts:

1. **Look for a platform with benefits.** You can find ETFs on many online investing platforms or through apps such as Robinhood. Check for platforms that offer commission-free trading so that you avoid paying transaction fees to these platforms.

2. **Take time to do research on ETFs.** That's right, you need to do some research. You can find a wide variety of ETFs in the market today, but they're not like individual securities. When you're deciding to invest in an EFT, you must consider the whole picture of the sector or industry that the EFT covers.

3. **Develop your trading strategy.** When starting out with ETF investments, consider using a dollar cost averaging approach. This way, you can spread out your investment into smaller amounts over time. This strategy

also acts to spread your returns over time, lessen the impact of market volatility, and ensure a disciplined approach.

Here are some real-life examples of ETFs:

- **SPDR S&P 500 (SPY)** tracks the S&P 500 and represents the oldest and most recognized ETF that's still around.
- **Invesco (QQQ)** indexes the (typically) technology stocks on the NASDAQ 100.
- **SPDR Dow Jones (DIA)** represents the Dow Jones exchange with its 30 industry stocks.
- **Sector ETFs** serve to track investments for single industries, for example, oil, energy, financial, or biotech industries.
- **Commodity ETFs** serve the commodities markets, which include commodities such as oil and gas.
- **Physically backed ETFs** follow goods such as gold or silver.

The EFT/Tax Relationship

Buying and selling transactions for an ETF mostly occur through an exchange. This makes the transactions more tax efficient than, for example, buying and selling through a mutual fund. With an ETF, there is no need for the sponsor to redeem or issue new shares for each transaction.

In the case of a mutual fund, investors can sell shares back to the fund and incur a tax liability that the shareholders of the fund must pay.

Whether it's a particular sector, a few particular companies, a cryptocurrency, or a real estate market, you will need to go deep on it and understand it better than most.

And you only have time, interest, energy, and attention to go deep on a few assets, so choose your income streams wisely.

Diversification may not lead to the highest level of portfolio income possible. But its goal is to protect your income and make you less likely to run into financial difficulty. So remember to grow and protect the income you earn through diversification.

Secrets of Multiple Streams of Income

From a young age, we are taught to think of having only *one* stream of income—a career. When you were asked, "What do you want to be when you grow up?" as a kid, can you imagine the look on adults' faces if you answered:

"I want to be an investor and business owner with a diverse portfolio of income-generating assets including passive-income businesses, interest- and dividend-paying securities, and real estate with good rental income, under management so I can set it and forget it."

It's unlikely many of the schoolteachers who asked you that question would even know what all of that meant—let alone how to help you put it into practice.

Since school didn't teach you—or even let you know about multiple streams of income, I'm here to fill in the gaps.

There are a few things we need to cover first:

1. Live within your means:

It is critically important to your financial future, and where you'll really see this pay off is in times of financial decline.

For many, many years in business, I wasn't netting millions, but what I was doing was investing half of what I made because I was living below my means. When you focus on being *wealthy* and not on "looking rich," you'll be able to live on less and invest more.

If you make it a habit to live on less than what you earn every single day in the good times, then you are more likely to get through the bad times. And you'll be less likely to rack up major debt, or have money issues in general, when gas prices go above six bucks a gallon or food prices increase 25%. Living within your means is going to prevent you from having to pay 19.95% interest on a credit card, which is a direct knife to the heart when building wealth.

2. Diversify your investments:

I always talk about putting 20% of your earned income into diversified investments. Why? Because if you have all of your money in one specific market, it's pretty easy that if you pick the wrong market, you're going to lose a lot of cash.

By not keeping all your money in a single investment, you can mitigate losses, which makes it less difficult to ride out a down economy or a market that's pulling back.

There are many ways to diversify your money—retirement accounts, real estate, metals, businesses. It's always good to have a portfolio with non-correlated investments. This means that if one investment (say, in stocks) is up, the other investment (perhaps in bonds) may be down (or vice versa).

In addition, consider adding investments that represent goods and businesses that are distinct from your primary job, business, or income stream. And just think, adopting these approaches to gaining financial security isn't just going to serve you in a recession or a down economy.

These approaches make for a solid strategy regardless of the market's state.

3. **Know the tolerance you have for risk:**

   Are you going to be up all night because your investments are down 17% this year even if the year has months to go? Maybe you should take a hard look at how your assets are distributed.

   Investments should give you a feeling of security, not increase your anxiety about finances. Knowing your risk tolerance and what type of investor you are will save you countless gray hairs and headaches.

4. **The 60/20/20 diversity rule:**

   The 60/20/20 diversity rule lets you leverage the outsized potential for profit from high-risk investments without risking being out on the street.

   In investing, it's not uncommon for a *great* investment to beat a *good* investment by 10X or even 100X. The problem is, the investments with the potential for 10X or 100X also have more of a chance of going to zero. This is because this upside potential is usually derived from some innovation, new trend, or new approach to business. And innovations and new trends are by definition unpredictable; you don't know how they're going to turn out. All you know is if they *do* turn out, they will turn out to be huge.

   But if you don't have a massive trust fund, which I'm guessing you don't, you don't want to risk being broke and destitute. More realistically, you don't want to risk countless sleepless nights hoping some volatile investment goes back up. That means you should never have all your eggs in the risky basket. I recommend sacrificing some upside potential in order to sleep better at night and to make sure you and your family are taken care of no matter what.

   That's why I recommend the **60/20/20 diversity rule:**

   > 60% in medium risk (market fluctuations are to be expected but stable long term);
   > 20% in high payoff, high risk (you might lose a little sleep over);
   > 20% in low payoff, low risk (it's so boring it makes you yawn).

   This gives you some diversification, but it allows you to go all in on what you think is a really strong investment. But no matter what, invest for the long term.

Markets are cyclical, but if you hold steady, you'll always have other chances to sell assets at a high price. Buying when the market is down, whether that is real estate or other investments is one of the best decisions you can make.

Now, that being said, if you're nearing 65, you may not want to take everything you have and go on high risk because you're going to need enough funds available from liquid, low-risk sources to retire when you want and be able to live off the interest. But if you want a few recession-proof investments, here's the way I look at things when the market starts to pull back.

Average Returns, Guaranteed—or Above-Average Returns with No Guarantee?

So you've got cash to invest now—what should you invest it in?
Your biggest questions to think about are:

Do you want average returns?
Or do you want the possibility of above-average returns, mixed with the possibility of below-average returns?

I'll bet your heart sank a little when you heard the first question. I mean who wants "average" returns? No one.

But there's an advantage to going for "average" returns in your retirement investment portfolio: They're virtually guaranteed. Think of how little else in your life is guaranteed!

If you can't stomach the thought of losing your hard-earned money by trying to chase the perfect buy, precisely time the market, or lose sleep over the volatility of your last buy—I get it.

Here is how your money can make money without taking the larger risk of chasing after "above average" returns.

Standard Practice

The standard—and therefore average—investment advice can be summarized easily as follows:

- Own a portfolio of widely diversified stocks in mutual funds, index funds, retirement accounts, or ETFs, mixed with some portion of bonds, moving more toward bonds the closer to retirement you are.
- Don't try to time the market.
- Never trade or sell—set it and forget it.

This "average" advice has almost always done very well for investors with horizons longer than a decade or two, so it's not stupid to bet that it will continue to do well. Your approach from a risk standard is lower than others. You'll always be in the same boat as everyone else, so you'll never be worse off than most people. This psychological factor actually counts for more than you might think, and this approach minimizes opportunities for regret.

Standard investing is more of a "peace of mind" approach.

More Aggressive Investing

What if you want to sacrifice "peace of mind" for the possibility of above-average returns?

> **Investing is a skill, just like running a business.**

You can be a great entrepreneur in your own industry and business and a below-average investor in other industries and businesses; the two don't necessarily go together.

However, given that you're reading this book, it's possible that you'll completely disregard the more "sensible" advice and seek out those above-average returns! (Risking big losses in the process!)

If you choose to ride these choppy waters in search of investment glory, I have a few time-tested pieces of advice:

1. **Take time to research and understand the market.** The only way you can get above-average returns in any asset is if you understand that asset far above the average player in that market.

   • Dig deeper than the average person;
   • Read and research more articles;
   • Consider more angles;
   • Talk to more people;
   • Do more homework;
   • Build relevant knowledge that gives you an edge.

   This is part of why many people can do well in local real estate.

   It's not wildly difficult to know more than most players in the local real estate market. You can gain lots of (legal) "insider" knowledge of what's hot and how things are trending just by walking around and talking to people. You can develop a feel for the market because you live in the market.

If you choose to pick individual stocks (most investment advisors will beg you not to do this), you have to fall in love with researching those stocks (like *I love* researching real estate).

2. **Invest more than money, invest time.**

If you're going to try to get above-average returns, you have to devote time and effort to the skill of investing, much like you have to devote time and resources if you want to play above-average music, above-average golf, or be an above-average entrepreneur.

It may make more sense to devote this time and effort to gaining above-average returns in your business—but it all depends on where you are currently within the w*ealth habits.*

No one can have an edge in everything. It's totally okay to make your nest egg safe and boring by putting it on autopilot, while you seek out the wildly above-average returns in your business. It all goes back to the type of investor you are or want to be.

3. **It's better to do one—or a few things really well—than to do every-thing just okay.**

A bulk of my money has been, is currently, and always will be in real estate. Yes, I have a portfolio of mutual funds, ETFs, crypto, and stocks, but I am heavy on what I know, what I study. And because of that knowledge, what I feel that I can control is real estate.

If you are okay to increase your risk, want to be more aggressive in investing, and go after above-average returns in some portion of your retirement/investment portfolio, just remember, we can't learn, understand, and research everything. As legendary billionaire investor Charlie Munger (Warren Buffett's right-hand man) says:

> ". . .A lot of people think that if they have 100 stocks, they're investing more professionally than they are if they have four or five. I regard this as absolute insanity. I think it's much easier to find five than it is to find 100. I think the people who argue for all this diversification, by the way, I call it 'diworsification,' which I copied from somebody. And I'm way more comfortable owning two or three stocks which I think I know something about and where I think I have an advantage" (La Roche, 2021).

As we continue to head into times of increasing market uncertainty, developing *wealth habits* is more important than ever.

Very few people saw the pandemic coming, the lockdowns, the Russian invasion of Ukraine, the supply-chain interruptions, and now inflation rearing its ugly head. Increased tension with China could even lead to even more supply-chain interruptions.

All of this goes to say, you never know where the next shock or surprise is going to come from. The best way to protect yourself from unpredictable economic shocks is to practice the *wealth habit* of multiple streams of income. If one stream of income dries up, you'll have several others to keep that financial water flowing into your wealth reservoir.

CHAPTER 7

The Three Reasons Why Owning a Business Is a Powerful Wealth-Builder

S tarting a business is one of the few pillars of wealth that has a low barrier of entry. You don't need an MBA, you don't need a million dollars to start, and you don't need some radical, life-changing idea. Regardless of where you are from, regardless of the education you have—entrepreneurship is for you.

Although you may not think of building a business as a form of wealth (compared to saving and investing in a Roth IRA for example), in fact, creating a small business is the primary way that most individuals and families build wealth in the United States. (The definition of wealth is simply the value of all assets of worth owned by a person, community, company, or country.)

Owning a business is a main driver of income generation and wealth accumulation among the top 10% and 1%. But what I love about business ownership is its role in wealth generation that's available for everyone.

Three Wealth Pillars

There are really three main pillars of wealth building—investments, real estate, and owning a business.

The first two of these pillars—investments and real estate—have either a high barrier to entry or a long time line to build wealth. And sometimes they have both.

Investing in mutual funds, Roth IRAs, a 401(k) has a low barrier to entry and a long time line.

Investing in real estate has a higher barrier to entry and the time line varies.

Starting a business, however, can be done in a weekend with very little money, and you can start generating income almost immediately.

There has really never been a better time to start a business. Technology has advanced so much that many businesses can be started with a laptop and an Internet connection.

The number of businesses that can be started with little to almost zero overhead is endless: consulting, marketing agency, membership communities, online digital products, media and PR company, graphic design, copywriting or editing services, mobile car detailing, photography or videography business, flipping products, recruiting or hiring agencies, pet sitting or dog walking, admin assistance/VA work, lawn care, freelancing on Fiverr or Upwork, financial planning, even software development—the list goes on.

There are three main reasons why owning a business is such a powerful wealth-builder: **cash flow, tax reduction, and asset creation.**

Let's unpack each of those a little more.

Cash Flow

Increasing the amount of money you make, your cash flow, by owning a business (even if you want or need to keep your job) will increase the amount you can invest and will result in you building wealth more quickly.

If you feel stuck, underemployed, or frustrated about the control you have over how much money you make, starting a business is a path to break free of this limitation as it has the potential for increased income and freedom.

In addition to adding another income stream, a business can also be an asset and one of the strongest ways to generate wealth.

But it isn't just about how much revenue you generate. You can have an eight-figure company and still go bankrupt.

It's all in the way you *manage* the money. The higher your profit margin in your business, the more profit you will be making. More profit = more money you get to keep.

Overall Tax Reduction

Depending on the business you start, it may take some time to turn a profit, but you can and should start taking advantage of tax breaks right off the bat. The government supports entrepreneurship and rewards those efforts with tax incentives such as deductions that reduce your taxable income. When you own a business, it offers opportunities to save on taxes. There are business tax deductions that you can optimize, and you can take advantage of unique retirement options available to you.

When you own a business you:

EARN MONEY → SPEND MONEY → PAY TAX

When you work for a business you:

EARN MONEY → PAY TAX → SPEND MONEY

Business owners get to use revenue before paying taxes while employees get their earnings taxed and have to live on the rest. This small shift creates a massive impact on your wealth.

Asset Creation

Owning a business gives you the ability to increase your equity, assets, and personal net worth.

An asset is anything that has current or future value. Essentially, assets include everything owned by the company that's currently valuable or could provide monetary benefit in the future. A business can have both— current value through profits and future value through profits and potentially an exit.

Equity in your business is all the assets less all the liabilities. If you were to close your business and liquidate, that equity would be what you have leftover for you. When you own your business, that equity also increases your personal net worth.

You have created an asset with your business, and that asset holds value. And if you run a successful business or create profitable cash flow, you can get the opportunity to sell your business and generate even more income.

Owning a Business Is a Key Wealth Habit

In *Rich Dad Poor Dad*, Robert Kiyosaki said that you shouldn't build a business (unless you really want to) to keep your job and buy real assets. And while I respect Robert and his teachings, I do have to disagree with him on this one. I've been building businesses on my own for almost 25 years now. I have the data and the real experience to tell you that business ownership is a much faster way to wealth.

If you're a teacher at a school, start a business. If you're a mechanic at a car dealership, start a business. If you're a marketing director for a corporation, start a business. If you're an attorney, a doctor, or a CPA, start a business.

Regardless of whether you like your job or hate it, you too can start a business. I'm not even suggesting you quit your job—yet. But let's break this down.

There's a stat that's been perpetuated in books, shared online, and talked about on stages (including by yours truly) that says, "Nine out of every 10 business start-ups fail in the first five years, and out of those that survive, nine out of every 10 of those will eventually fail too." And it's true. But you can do a few things to hedge those numbers in your favor.

The Safest Route

If you have fear about starting a new business, know you're not alone. The most common thing that holds people back from becoming an entrepreneur isn't lack of a plan or lack of an idea—it's fear.

Fear of failure, fear of other people's opinions, fear of success (yes, it's a thing)—but you don't have to take a huge giant leap to start, you just have to take the first step.

A huge giant leap would be to quit your job, leverage your entire savings, sell your house, burn the boats, and "go all in"! You commonly hear that shared on the insta-feeds of social media, but depending on your current situation, and your current responsibilities, that opinion may be reckless.

The safest route to starting a business is doing it while keeping the job you already have. The reason that most businesses fail—the nine out of every 10—is because people start businesses in areas they don't have any expertise or experience in the industry they chose. Or they haven't done any market research to find out whether their business is needed and people (customers) will buy from them.

The safest route to building a business is to look for the 4-Way Business Intersection.

- **What you know** (ability to deliver; what you have knowledge, skills, or experience in);
- **What people will buy** (market need);
- **What you can sell** (products or services that can generate revenue);
- **What you want** (the purpose of the business).

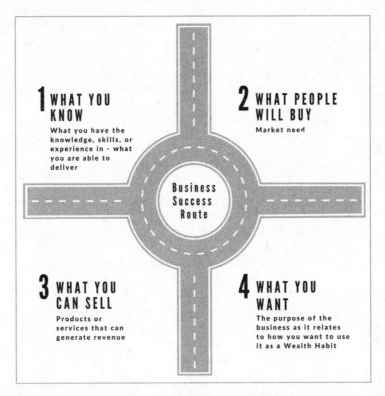

Of course, you can start a business a million other ways depending on the capital you have, connections or relationships you've built, and the idea or plan you have, but how you can start today, right now, is as simple as following the steps above.

Just about anyone can start a business doing exactly what they do in their job but doing it for themselves. This is called being self-employed, or a freelancer/solopreneur in more recent terms. Regardless of what you call it, you keep your existing job and work your business in addition to your regular work hours. This gives you the ability to earn additional money, and it opens you up to everything I'm talking about in this book—tax deductions, the best retirement plans, additional streams of income, and *earning* more so that you can *invest* more.

Starting a business even if you have no plans on leaving your job could be one of the best decisions you ever make for your financial future. Although the main reason people don't start a business is because they are afraid to fail. However, did you know that more than 75% of all millionaires in America own their own businesses? So rather than worrying about why you might fail, how about this question: **What if you succeed?**

When I work with entrepreneurs all over the world, I often ask this question when they are trying to figure out what type of business they should start, or even if they should try to diversify their income stream and create additional programs, products, and services for their existing business.

So let me ask you a question. This question may seem simple but the answer can be quite profound. Take a few minutes right now to pause and answer.

If you knew you couldn't fail and your success was guaranteed, what would you do?

_____

_____

_____

_____

_____

_____

_____

_____

_____

_____

_____

_____

The answer to that question is going to give you major insight to what your next step should be.

But before you take your next step, you need to be sure what your next step _isn't_. That's what the next chapter is all about.

CHAPTER 8

Calling Out the BS in Business—and How to Avoid It

Did you get your BS in business?

And no, I don't mean a bachelor of science degree.

Unfortunately, if you've scrolled through "entrepreneur" Instagram or watched enough YouTube videos on business, you've probably heard more than enough to earn a degree in business BS!

Many of the ideas you hear online come from people who have never actually built a business before. At most, many of the business "gurus" are in their first business—teaching people how to build a business who are teaching people how to build a business—and the huge, glaring thing that's lacking is any *actual* real-world business experience.

When you get misinformation from that guy who is leasing a house, buying a new car, or just rented a private jet for a few hours all while showing you the "dream life" in insta-stories to look like he's "made it," not only does that misinformation fail to inform you of anything valuable—it actually *costs you*. It costs you money, time, focus, and energy by following the wrong advice from the wrong people.

So before I start breaking down the mechanics of business, I first want to bust through some of these "philosophies" you may have heard about and explain why they don't work.

BS #1: Follow Your Passion

Okay, so let's get this out of the way. I am not one of those people who says, "Follow your passion, and the money will come."

I am not suggesting you build a business you hate. But this philosophy of "love what you do every day" is garbage. It's an old, overused cliché that's been regurgitated over and over across social media feeds, self-help books, seminar stages, and even touted by "coaches" with no research or context. And, quite frankly, it is not very good advice.

Ultimately, this is the message that could be holding you back from actually moving forward. Building a business, or a career, around a passion sets you up for failure. Hear me out.

According to not one, not two, but *three* Stanford researchers' findings, this "follow your passion" BS advice can be detrimental to your success (Hess, 2018).

Here's the science on why "follow your passion" is bad advice:

1. **The statement implies we have one passion.** I don't know anyone who is passionate about one singular thing. Ask any parent what they are passionate about, and they'll say their kids; ask any dog lover what they are passionate about, and they will say their dog—that doesn't mean you want to start a business around kids or dogs. People have more than one interest, and selecting just one passion narrows your focus and prevents other ideas from being uncovered.

2. **It assumes people, and their passions, don't change with time.** We continually evolve in every stage of our lives. What you are passionate about and love to do in your 20s will not likely be the same in your 40s. We are constantly changing, and that means our passions will likely change too.

3. **It implies we already know what our passion is.** Many people have no clue what their passion is, let alone how they can tie it to a business. Nor should you. If this is you, you're not alone. You need time, exploration, and exposure to many different things in life before you're able to even know what you're even passionate about. Trying to tie your life's

work to your passion is an instant source of stress and anxiety. And then you think something is wrong with you because you haven't found "your passion" yet. (P.S. There isn't anything wrong with you.)

4. **Just because you have a passion for something, doesn't mean you are good at it, nor does it mean you can monetize it.** I may be passionate about singing, but it doesn't mean I'm any good at it. So imagine I build a business or career around singing, but no one hires me because I suck. If you aren't good at your chosen passion, you're unlikely to make money at it, which will ultimately be frustrating and defeating.

5. **Lastly, the glaring flashing sign most people miss: If you shift your passion into a job, it becomes just that—work.** If you take doing something you love and turn it into something for monetary gain, your passion may very well lose the feeling it once had. No matter what business or job you have, there are going to be days you are not passionate about working with that client, handling that employee, or running that webinar. A passion can be a hobby instead of a profession.

Passions Are Developed, Not Chased After

It's time to flip the worn-out script and bad advice of "follow your passion". Passions are developed, not chased after. Build a business that generates money so you can have what everyone wants—time and freedom—then you can follow any passion you want.

Find What Energizes You and What Drains You

Discovering what lights you up, and realizing what doesn't, will be far more valuable in aligning your path with success. The goal should be to build a business and a life that aligns with who you are *and* what you can be successful at. If you enjoy what you do, you will be able to outrun, outlast, and out-survive anyone in your industry.

THE BATTERY TENDER

There are things that you do every day that either **CHARGE** your internal battery, and there are things that you do every day that **DRAIN** it. This exercise will help you identify and sort your daily tasks/duties/job requirements to gain clarity and insight into both to help you live a more **ENERGIZED** life!

ENERGIZING

The things, tasks, or even people you list here are things that light you up, are easy to work on or create, and make you feel better, light, happy, or fulfilled.

DRAINING

The things, tasks, or even people you list here are things that you dread, procrastinate on, are not easy to work on or create, and make you feel worse, heavy, irritated, or angry.

_____
_____
_____
_____
_____
_____
_____
_____
_____
_____

_____
_____
_____
_____
_____
_____
_____
_____
_____
_____

GOAL: Once you identify things that **ENERGIZE** your battery, find ways to do more of them! How could you set up your life or work so that you are doing **MORE** of these types of activities on a daily basis? What could you eliminate in order to have more time to do more of this? What tasks can you delegate to give you space for more of these?

GOAL: Once you identify things that **DRAIN** your battery, decide if they are things you can **CHANGE** or if you have to change your VIEW of them. If it's something you're able to change, ask yourself, "How can I **eliminate. delegate, or automate** this?" If you can't change it (e.g. paying taxes), ask yourself, "How can I view this more positively?"

BS #2: You Don't Need a Plan— Just Start!

Look, I'm all for starting before you feel ready. In fact, I say it is required because when you're starting something new, you'll never feel ready. It can also be great advice if the problem you're having is that you have a great idea, but you are over-complicating it or simply afraid to fail, so you delay it to avoid the risk.

Perfectionism is the death of an idea, so I think most people mean well when they say, "Just start, don't over-plan and research forever"—and for that it is good advice. The push *can* work really well, although it can also be detrimental without context.

Because like I shared above, the fact remains that 91% of all businesses fail. And what's one of the most common reasons why? Failure to plan.

We focus so hard on getting things done. We're busy checking off our to-do lists, collecting accomplishments, feeling productive—but failing to take the time to do the silent and seemingly unproductive work of planning (to be certain that what you want to develop will work as you intend) is critical to your success.

We create results not by what we start but through what we can sustain.

Taking the time to plan, pausing to think about what you are about to do, reflecting on whether it's a journey you should take is all time well spent.

It is not about how quickly you can start, it's about how long you can sustain. And for that you need a plan. Planning provides speed, competitive advantages, confidence, direction, and flexibility to adapt when challenges arise. There is nothing more defeating than feeling like you have no clarity, no direction, and ending up like a hamster on a wheel running and running but getting nowhere. Because when you measure "starting" as the indicator of success you won't be able to sustain success in any area of life.

Success requires a plan, acting on that plan every day, and gaining more clarity about the process so you can move with greater speed—that is what will lead you to long-term sustainability.

BS #3: Do Everything Yourself

I see so many early-stage entrepreneurs make the mistake of doing everything themselves. It is true that in the beginning of business, you need to save where you can, which includes doing things yourself, especially until you are out of the conceptual stage of your business. But more often than not, business owners do that for too long, and it ends up costing them a lot of money. Focusing on the motto "Every penny matters" for too long will create half-assed results, and subpar returns. Part of growing good business practices includes recognizing when you can't do everything yourself. And although money matters, knowing when to hire outside resources is a critical skill to acquire.

Being in business for as long as I have and then coming into this online world of business was almost shocking to me. People are teaching hopeful new entrepreneurs to learn all about creating their own Facebook ads, how to create their own marketing funnels, how to design their own website, how to pitch their own PR. And while it is good to have an understanding of all those mechanisms—if you try to do all of that yourself, you are left with no time to focus on the actual product or service you offer.

The next three sections outline the reasons why doing everything yourself, or trying to, is a bad idea for growth.

1. **Revisiting the concept of opportunity cost:**

   I talked about opportunity costs in Chapter 5, and the concept absolutely applies here. Remember that everything in business is associated with an opportunity cost. Don't make the mistake of devaluing your time and attention. Like most entrepreneurs, I am sure you are very talented and could potentially do a lot of things yourself. However, is it worth your time? That's a question to ask. And here's the magical key to the kingdom I want you to remember: **Just because you *can* do something, doesn't mean you *should*.**

   One of the common mistakes entrepreneurs make in the beginning is trying to get things done for cheap, cutting corners, and trying to do everything themselves. They think they are actually saving money; however, doing tasks you can otherwise delegate and hire out is actually *costing* you money.

   The tricky part with opportunity cost is: It's an unseen expense. It's what a person sacrifices when they make one choice over another. The main challenge of opportunity cost in business? It is an invisible liability that doesn't show up on your business statements making it easy to overlook.

2. **Recognizing that you're probably not good at everything:**

Suppose that you have amazing marketing skills but fall a bit short when it comes to customer service. That situation just points to the fact that you can't be the best person for every job in the business. Consider the athletic performance that led Michael Jordan (one of the greatest basketball players ever) to attempt a second career in another major league sport. The second career didn't go so well. Don't remember what that was? Me either. (I had to look it up! It was baseball.)

But it does land the point that no one is great at everything. It's important to outsource and hire others who have strengths that complement the areas in which you have weaknesses—or with tasks that are simply not the best use of your time.

Here is a quick formula on how to figure out whether you should outsource or hire someone to do that task:

1. Take the amount of money you earn in a year _____

   (You can do this monthly or weekly if you have a job and earn a salary. If you have a business, it is easier to take your net profit from an income statement, and factor in owner's draws or wages you take over a 12-month period so you get an average.)

2. Divide by the number of hours you work in that same time period

   _____

   (e.g. $50,000 a year divided by 52 weeks divided by 40 hours, or less if you work this part time.)

3. You get _____ dollars per hour

   Hire or outsource any task you can (in your business or your life!) for the same or less hourly rate than the number above.

This is how you free up more time to focus on the things that will give you more time, more focus, and enable you to make you more money.

For example, if you make $50,000 a year:

$50,000 / 52 weeks a year $961.53 a week / 40 hours = $24.04 / hr.

If you could hire someone to do your house cleaning, landscaping, laundry, and make appointments for you (non-income building activities), it could be a smart investment for you to outsource those things so you can spend your time doing income-building activities.

This is your permission slip to hire the people you need to hire—it doesn't matter how big or small, delegate the jobs you can so you can have extra time to spend on your business or building something alongside your current job.

The same thing goes once you have a business. I can't tell you how many entrepreneurs I work with still handle tasks such as administrative, website updates, trying to learn how to run a Facebook Ad, or figure out how to build a funnel.

Every minute you spend trying to learn those things and not delegate them, you're taking time and money out of your business account as opposed to saving. It would be far easier to spend an hour and find somebody who can do those things than it is to try and develop the talents and skills to do it yourself.

This also frees up space in your day, your mind, and your focus for you to do more of what you do best. Nothing will increase your productivity and your bottom line, i.e. your money, faster than delegating tasks that you really shouldn't be performing.

3. **Making your ability to focus into a valuable commodity:**

Any multitasker knows that being pulled in too many directions can negatively impact effectiveness. Of course, the idea of multitasking itself presents problems. When tasks involve thinking, human brains can't really handle two separate tasks at one time. Instead, brains switch back and forth rapidly between tasks, working sequentially and making us believe that we're multitasking. We're actually skipping around, and if the tasks are demanding, we're probably underperforming.

Pair this situation with today's modern technologies that put additional demands on our attention and focus. The rise of personal communications and computing devices—developed to supposedly help us simplify—actually increase the amount of information vying for our attention (by as much as four to five times since 1980). These distractions also impact our productivity and, most likely, our results.

And so, learning to pay attention and focus on the tasks at hand becomes a most valuable business commodity.

Here are a few ways to improve your focus:

• **Focus on importance:** Use your concentration and energy on whatever is most vital. Don't be afraid to dismiss irrelevant information, and focus on the most important tasks and projects first. According to *The Productive Engineer* blog, "Research shows that people who execute their most difficult tasks first are generally more productive and high achieving than those who start easy and work their way up".

- **Improve your attention:** Make a list of priorities. Not all tasks are created equal, and using my **productivity grid** will help you capture everything you need. By breaking down complex projects into smaller tasks that you can move forward, it will help you feel like your completion rate is high (the feeling we receive from easy tasks) while still accomplishing the challenging opportunities and priorities.

Here is the Productivity Grid Framework:

CAPTURE & COLLECT

Step 1: You have to capture and collect all of those thoughts. The ideas swirling around in your head are not only taking up space in that brain of yours, but they're also distracting you. Capture and collect all of those ideas—regardless of what they might be. You have to get all of those thoughts out of your head and onto paper.

CATEGORIZE

Category:
- ☐ _____
- ☐ _____
- ☐ _____
- ☐ _____
- ☐ _____
- ☐ _____

Category:
- ☐ _____
- ☐ _____
- ☐ _____
- ☐ _____
- ☐ _____
- ☐ _____

Category:
- ☐ _____
- ☐ _____
- ☐ _____
- ☐ _____
- ☐ _____
- ☐ _____

Category:
- ☐ _____
- ☐ _____
- ☐ _____
- ☐ _____
- ☐ _____
- ☐ _____

Category:
- ☐ _____
- ☐ _____
- ☐ _____
- ☐ _____
- ☐ _____
- ☐ _____

Category:
- ☐ _____
- ☐ _____
- ☐ _____
- ☐ _____
- ☐ _____
- ☐ _____

Step 2: Once you have captured and collected all of those thoughts and gathered them on paper, you run them through the productivity grid and categorize them.

You may have a category for your business or work, a project, or goal you're working toward and even one for personal things. The goal is to break down all the individual items you captured and collected and sort through each. Determine what's actually needed, what's really not, and to find tasks and responsibilities that are like each other and add them together in one section.

This is part of the exact process I have used to run multiple companies, build a nonprofit, manage numerous real estate projects, keep my health in check—and what has helped me accomplish massive goals in otherwise "impossible" time lines.

You can find the entire four-step process at: **www.candyvalentino.com**.

- **Limit distractions:**

You can minimize interruptions in a few ways:

  - Turn your phone on focus mode and flip it upside down;
  - Turn off notifications on your computer, tablet, or whatever you're working on;
  - If you can't be disciplined enough to limit your time on social media, delete the app.

If you look at your phone or device every time a text, email, or app notification pops up, your productivity will be so low your efficiency won't even be at 20% throughout the day. A research study conducted at the University of California, Irvine, found that, on average, it takes around **23 minutes** for most workers to get back on task after an interruption (Schramm, 2021).

- **Beware of procrastination:**

If something isn't a priority right now, then focusing on it right now is a waste of time and a way that you're procrastinating on the tasks that need your time and attention. Handle the most important tasks first and schedule less important priorities toward the end of the day.

- **Minimize substances:**

"Alcohol takes over 24 hours to leave our body, and when it does, it leaves us feeling more anxious, further challenging our ability to focus" (Clark, n.d). Excess caffeine creates overstimulation, which also limits your ability to focus. And a new study carried out by University College London (UCL) has found that marijuana use has a major effect on the way that our brains process information and reduces a person's short-term motivation. Minimizing substances will maximize your focus, your results, and, ultimately, your income.

- **Exercise:**

   "Studies show that as little as 20 minutes of aerobic exercise will increase your ability to concentrate and focus" (Clark, n.d). Personally, when I follow the above ways to focus and still can't get into a rhythm, exercise is the game changer for me. If I ever feel like I'm hitting a wall, 20 to 30 minutes of even a brisk walk outside radically shifts my energy and gets me back into the frame of focus.

> ## When you try focusing on everything, you end up not focusing on anything.

BS #4: Find Your Purpose

I hate to say it, but I have to say it: "Go find your purpose" is just like "Follow your passion." It's terrible advice. (Like we need another way to make us feel as if we are lacking and think we need something else that we don't have.)

The whole idea of finding your purpose leaves out one really important fact: where you are right *now*. Many of the most inspiring and purpose-driven people I know do very ordinary things with an extraordinary perspective.

Some people will tell you "your purpose" is your dream job or dream business. But purpose is not a job. It's not even something you have to *find* because purpose is not an achievement. The danger is that when we tell people to "go find" their purpose, they end up mentally neglecting the present. Often fantasizing about some future epiphany that will magically reveal their purpose to them.

The constant state of focusing on something you don't have while consciously or unconsciously searching to find or discover it creates a lack of clarity and a feeling of anxiety and overwhelm. You cannot "find" your purpose because you've never lost it. You already have purpose by default.

Instead of "finding purpose," how about we live with purpose.

People find many ways to live with purpose, and the following are a few common traits of those who do:

1. **They live in the present:**

   The biggest contradiction in "find your purpose" is that it is the complete opposite of being in the present—the actual definition of purposeful. The core of the purposeful-living concept contains the idea that all things happen to us for a reason. Experiencing hardship shows us what we need to learn and gives us an opportunity to grow. A less-than-ideal outcome (in our eyes) may indicate that we need to open ourselves to new options or outcomes that we wouldn't otherwise choose.

2. **They connect the dots:**

Realize that everything you've been through has brought you to this moment. Every challenge you've faced and every struggle you've been through was orchestrated for your greatest learning. When we are able to look back and connect the dots of everything that brought us to this very place, we're able to be present and find purpose in even the mundane.

Rather than focusing on the task you're doing at the moment, ask yourself, **What is the greater vision it is serving?** Are you working a full-time job and starting a business to build more wealth and have more time with your kids? Are you picking up extra clients and work because you want to go on more trips and create more memories? Whatever it is for you, focusing on the greater vision of *why* you're doing it and not the work or action in the moment—connecting the dots—will keep you tied to living more purposely.

3. **They serve others:**

Consider the characteristics of two businesses, both of which make and distribute their own clothing line. The first business uses renewable or recycled materials (no animal products) and pays livable wages to its employees. The second business expends considerable time and energy gathering unused raw materials, includes animal fur in its designs, and employs slave laborers. The first business enriches the community and serves others; the second business only takes and offers no service. Whether you create a business that serves, volunteer for a cause you care about, help ease the struggles of others, or assist victims of abuse or disaster, remember that finding fulfillment and purpose puts service to others at the forefront.

BS #5: This Next Great Idea Will Make Me Rich

Ideas are so overrated. Look, I'm all for big ideas and dreaming big, but it's just one part of the whole picture.

Everywhere you go someone has a million-dollar idea. A business or product that is going to change the world, an idea that's going to be a billion-dollar brand. And while I appreciate the optimism, executing on that idea is a massive task.

Ideas are cheap, easy, and they are a dime a dozen. You can come up with hundreds, but you only have time to implement a few because ideas don't build companies. Ideas won't create millions of dollars in sales and generate wealth for you and your family—it's the implementation and execution of those ideas that do.

How many times have you heard someone say, "I thought of this invention idea and so-and-so stole my idea." Sorry, Fred, they didn't steal your idea. They just did what you failed to do—execute.

> **Ideas won't build a successful business, but the implementation and execution of those ideas will.**

That's because most modern-day entrepreneurs are in love with ideation, but few are disciplined enough for implementation. They will have an idea, talk all about it, and when they see someone doing what they had in mind, you'll hear, "I once had this idea" or "This person stole my idea." This leaves so much opportunity for *you* to be successful.

Let's say I have finally convinced you, and you are going to make the leap to either leave your job and build a business or create a business while keeping your job.

We need to get into some of the boring yet important and simple steps to actually building a business. This is where the rubber meets the road. And I'm excited to jump in—let's go.

CHAPTER 9

Yes, You Can Start a Business—Here's How

Now that you know what to *avoid* in business—let's focus on how to *actually* build a business.

After building several businesses of my own—in various industries over the last 25 years—and now working with founders, business owners, and entrepreneurs in every industry imaginable, I have done the research and have the actual experience on what it takes to build a successful, scalable, and sustainable business.

This chapter will get you started. It's certainly not a complete guide to business—I will be writing that book soon enough—but it's enough to get you inspired, point you in the right direction, and show you the initial path you'll take.

Ready to join me?

Nine Initial Steps to Starting a Business

There are far more than nine steps to getting started in business, and although that is a whole book in itself—there are a few parts I specifically want to cover.

They are: defining its purpose, doing your research, choosing your business structure, getting a federal tax ID number, opening a business account, obtaining a business credit card, business funding, financial software, and protecting your name.

Let's run through each of these nine steps.

1. Define the Purpose

This does not mean, "Go find your life's purpose."☺

This is understanding the purpose of the *business*—it is important to know why you are starting. You must describe the reason/purpose for starting a business to begin with.

Differentiate between whether the business serves a personal need or a need in the market. If the purpose of the business is to serve a personal need—income diversification, tax benefits, earning more—it will be built with that in mind.

On the other hand, if you're building a business to fill a need in the market and you want to be an entrepreneur for the rest of your life, the *scope* of what you need to build will be much different and of course much bigger.

The purpose is simply the reason you have formed your business boiled down to a single sentence or two. This isn't your mission or vision and doesn't need to be anything complex. Keep it simple, short and, straightforward.

If you're unclear, here are a couple questions to ask yourself:

- Do you want to run a business, or do you enjoy doing the work you do?
- Do you want to be self-employed and work for yourself, or do you want to build a team and create a big company?
- What makes this business unique?
- What does the business plan on selling?

What's the main reason you're starting a business (or why have you created it)?

_____

_____

_____

One of my secrets to really being able to accomplish anything is this: **Start with the end in mind.** Reverse engineer your desired outcome. The only way you know *how* to move forward is to first know *what* you are moving toward. Not understanding the purpose of your business is like getting in your car and starting to drive—only you have no idea what the destination is. How will you know if you get there if you have no idea where you're going?

Tip: Some states require a business purpose statement when filing for an LLC. This statement is often included with the Articles of Organization.

2. Do Your Research

Just about every study shows that one of the contributing reasons most businesses fail is failure to plan. But when businesses do plan, the only reason those plans fail are because they are often filled with bad ideas. Grand ideas seem great—until you figure out that the market doesn't actually want or need your product (or you have failed at learning how to manufacture or distribute your product). To make sure that a business idea is sound, entrepreneurs need to do their research before spending a lot of time and money on a project.

It may seem like common knowledge to say that before starting a business, but let's cover a few things and hedge the odds in your favor.

Ensure you can do the primary work of the business.

Can you build a business in an industry that you have no experience or skill in? Sure you can. But it's much, much harder, and it has been proven that it increases your risk of failure.

Let's look through the next 14 questions below and learn how doing your business research and taking a little time to plan can often reduce the common yet avoidable mistakes that lead to a large number of business failures.

1. Is there a demand for this product or service? _____

    _____

2. Do you have expertise or experience in this area? _____

    _____

3. What equipment, supplies, and inventory do you need? _____

    _____

4. How many employees do you need to deliver your product/service? _____

    _____

5. What products and services do you sell? _____

    _____

6. Who are your ideal customers? _____

    _____

7. Who is your ideal customer, where do they live, what do they do, what social platforms do they engage with, etc.? _____

    _____

8. What are the values of your business, and what does it stand for? _____

   _____

9. How will you market and promote your business? _____

   _____

10. Where are your customers located? _____

    _____

11. Do you need any resources or funding to start? _____

    _____

12. How can you differentiate your business from your competition? _____

    _____

13. What is your financial/funding plan? _____

    _____

14. Is e-commerce an important aspect of your business, or will your sales be in-person? _____

    _____

These are all questions you'll want to ask yourself and take some time to answer. There is no reason to develop some lengthy, elaborate business plan that takes years to complete—and will be quickly out of date—but you want to do some research and ask these core questions. You don't need to plan every detail in your business, but you do need to prepare your business for success.

3. Business Structure

One of the most important decisions is how to structure your business. Your business structure affects how much you pay in taxes, your ability to raise money, the paperwork you need to file, and how much personal liability you're taking on.

It's important to know these things because as I have worked with entrepreneurs and business owners over the years, I have seen those doing $500,000 and even over a million in revenue yet they have the wrong business structure in place.

We are going to cover the common four structures. I have an online course with in-depth breakdowns, how the taxes work, as well as the advantages and disadvantages of each. It's way more advanced than we can or need to cover here, but I wanted to make sure you have an understanding of each.

Sole Proprietorship

This is the simplest and most common structure entrepreneurs choose because most people start without knowing the things I'm going to break down here. I'll sum up this structure in two words: *high risk*.

In short, there is no distinction between the business and the owner. You are entitled to all profits and are responsible for all your business's debts, losses, and liabilities. Most new business owners become sole proprietors because there is no formal action required to form one. Because you and your business are one and the same, the business itself is not taxed separately—the sole proprietorship income is your income.

Partnerships

This is the simplest structure for two or more people to own a business together. A general partnership has similar risk to that of a sole proprietor, but there are two common kinds of partnerships: limited partnerships (LP) and limited liability partnerships (LLP).

Partnerships can be a good choice for businesses with multiple owners, professional groups such as attorneys, doctors, accountants, etc.

Partnerships tend to have the most complications should a business relationship go south. Even if you have a solid exit strategy in your partnership agreement, changes in your partners' situations can cause issues, so always make sure to consult with an attorney.

Corporations—C and S Corp

A corporation, sometimes called a C corp, offers the strongest protection to its owners from personal liability, but the cost to form a corporation is higher than other structures and also requires more extensive record-keeping, operational processes, and reporting. In some cases, corporate profits are taxed twice—first, when the company makes a profit, and again when dividends are paid to shareholders on their personal tax returns. That's why this structure has been dubbed the "double-taxation corporation."

An S corporation is a special election that you file with the IRS. It avoids the double taxation drawback of regular C corps.

S corps allow profits, and some losses, to be passed through directly to owners' personal income without being subject to corporate tax rates. The S corp protects you from personal liability that can cause you to lose your personal wealth in assets such as your home, car, or savings and its flow-through taxation helps reduce your tax burden. There are additional fees to set up and maintain, so you want to make sure you consult with your tax professional to make sure the S-corp election is a good fit for you and your business.

LLC—Limited Liability Company

An LLC lets you take advantage of the benefits of both the corporation and partnership business structures. It protects you from personal liability in most instances, your personal assets—such as your vehicle, house, and savings accounts—and lowers your risk in case your LLC faces bankruptcy or lawsuits.

Profits and losses can get passed through to your personal income without facing corporate taxes. Because of the flow-through taxation, profits are taxed at the member's personal tax level and avoid double taxation. But unlike an S corp, in an LLC all income may be subject to payroll or self-employment taxes.

Choose your business structure carefully. While you may convert to a different business structure in the future, there may be restrictions based on your location. This could also result in tax consequences and unintended dissolution, among other complications.

What is right for you as you are starting out may not be the structure that the mature version of your business needs. Always consult with your business attorney and accountant as they can be helpful in this process.

4. Get a Federal Tax ID (EIN number)

A business EIN is the equivalent of a person's Social Security Number (SSN). It makes your business legit with the federal government. If your business is located in the United States or US Territories, you can go to: **www.irs.gov** to apply for an EIN online. The person applying online must have a valid Taxpayer Identification Number (SSN, ITIN, EIN). Best of all, it only takes a few minutes to apply and receive your EIN.

5. Open a Business Checking Account

Take the EIN number from your newly formed entity and open a business checking account. Developing a relationship with a business banker will help you as your business grows. If you have a regional or local banker in your area, that's always a great place to start as it may be easier to form a relationship. Your business banker will be a great resource should you need loans, a line of credit, or merchant services for your business.

Remember, having a separate business checking account is critical. You don't ever want to mix business funds with personal funds in the same account as it can put your personal assets at risk.

6. Get a Business Credit Card

Apply for a separate business credit card. A business credit card will continue the separation between you and your business and will also help maintain risk protection. Use this new card to make every purchase for your business, and set up all business-related subscriptions such as software, marketing subscriptions, and other recurring charges to this card. Most likely, you don't want to get this from your bank.

The options for credit cards are endless and can even be fun to research. As you make monthly business purchases on this card, you will accrue reward points or cash back. I always say to find a card with a rewards program that aligns with you and what you enjoy. Disney—to take the family on vacation. Delta—to get priority access for travel and free flights. Marriott—to get status at their hotels and free stays. There are so many options, but in my opinion, the best one to get is American Express. American Express is a charge card meaning it doesn't give you a credit limit and needs to be paid in full every month. As long as you're disciplined with spending, it is an incredible card with flexibility.

Whichever you choose, be diligent with spending and set the autopay amount to pay in full every month so you aren't racking up unnecessary and wealth-draining interest charges.

7. Business Funding

There are a variety of ways to get funding for your business (if you need it). Generally speaking, some of the main ones are:

1. Business loan: The Small Business Association (SBA) has incredible programs for business owners; learn more by going to: **www.sba.gov**.

2. Crowdfunding: It is a way of raising funds that enables you to collect money from a large number of people via online platforms. Crowdfunding is most often used by start-up companies or growing businesses. These platforms include Kickstarter, Indiegogo, Fundable, Fundly, and SeedInvest—each of their websites has more information.

3. Investors: You can seek investments from friends and family, or get investors. Investors come in a variety of flavors—silent partners may invest without active participation while others may want to be actively involved. An angel investor may want to be involved for a short period and then cash out. Venture capital (VCs) investors have specific goals, objectives, and expectations. Just remember: Investors create responsibilities.

4. Line of credit: If you own any property, you can apply for a line of credit (LOC/HELOC, home equity line of credit). It allows you to draw funds as you need them and typically offers a great interest rate. It uses your property as collateral to leverage debt and can help finance a business venture.

5. Net terms or leasing. Working with companies who allow 30/60/90 days for payments or leasing equipment could give you some help on purchasing inventory or business equipment needed.

8. Financial Software

Bookkeeping is a critical step to any business, regardless of which structure you're in. You can't take the proper deductions, evaluate your numbers, or receive an accurate picture of your business finances without it. I will always recommend QuickBooks as it is the industry standard, and all accountants can work with it. However, there are less expense options out there as well. Just make sure whichever one you choose is one that your CPA will use and can grow with your business as you grow.

9. Protect Your Name

If you operate under a name different than your own, you will most likely have to file a fictitious name (also known as an assumed name, trade name, or DBA, short for "doing business as," name). Depending on the business you're in, and what products or services you offer, you may consider trademarks or other types of legal protection, especially if you have intellectual property.

I have an expanded version of this—a 25 step-by-step checklist every business owner needs—along with other valuable business resources at: **www.candyvalentino.com**.

Now that you know how to get started in your business, it's time for one of the parts of business that is most exciting: earning revenue!

CHAPTER 10

Real-World Business Lessons on Revenue Growth

You are ready to start a business or grow one that you currently have. But how do you actually *make* money? (Or more of it?!)

I've worked with founders doing hundreds of thousands of dollars in revenue and others doing hundreds of millions in revenue, and no matter what stage of business you're in, entrepreneurs are always focused on growth. Because it's one thing to start a business, but it's another thing to consistently grow your revenue and maintain profitability.

You can spend countless hours working on a great idea or perfecting the product or service you offer in your business, but success in business is determined by this—your ability to acquire customers, generate sales, and maintain profitability. You can't have a business without the first two, and you can't stay in business without the third.

Acquiring new customers may sound simple, but depending on the business you're in, it can be challenging to find new opportunities in today's marketplace. If you don't stay up to date and tweak your marketing strategies, you may struggle to keep your sales funnel full.

But when you break down all the brilliance of business titans and simplify all the strategies that work for the best of the best in their industries, believe it or not, there are only four ways to increase your revenue. There are of course numerous ways that you can execute each of them, but when you simplify business growth at its core all roads lead back to these four revenue growth principles:

Real-World Revenue Growth

Growth #1: Customer Acquisition— Increase the Number of Your Total Customers

Customer acquisition refers to bringing in new customers—people who buy your products or services. It is a process used to bring potential customers down the marketing funnel from brand awareness to make a purchasing decision.

Customer acquisition involves a mix of marketing, media, and engagement (lead generation and product offerings) to gain new customers through targeting them and reaching them through online and offline customer journeys.

Some of the ways to acquire more customers are through:

- SEO optimization;
- Content marketing;
- Affiliate marketing;
- Digital advertising;
- Traditional advertising (print, TV, radio);
- Trade shows;
- Direct mail;
- Email;
- Social media campaigns;
- Events;
- PR and media.

According to Masterclass.com, "Customer acquisition is the process by which a business converts potential customers into paying customers" (Masterclass, 2022). The customer acquisition process is typically broken up into three phases: **awareness, interest/consideration, purchase.**

Customer acquisition strategies will vary depending on the business you're in, but they're generally built around these three phases.

Phase 1: Lead Generation and Awareness

The first phase of the customer acquisition involves generating brand awareness. How will you reach your potential customers? This can be through direct mail, media and TV advertising, digital marketing, social media, Facebook and TikTok ads, and direct mail. Until you know exactly where to obtain your new customers from, using a mix of acquisition channels to test each will expose potential customers to your brand, creating awareness about your products or services.

Where does your customer "live"?

This is a question you want to ask yourself (or collect the data from your customers once you have them). Are they on Facebook? on TikTok? Do they watch a streaming service? Are you able to purchase a mailing list and send them direct mail? Are they at trade shows? Where does your target customer "live"?

_____

_____

Phase 2: Prompt Interest and Encourage Consideration

The second step focuses on providing more information to customers who are aware of your brand but encourages them to make a buying decision. This can be done through SEO, retargeting ads, email marketing—this phase encourages email list signup, sales call inquiries, and engagement. The more informed potential customers are, the more likely they are to make a purchasing decision.

What can you implement that will move new customers into phase 2 and encourage them to consider purchasing from you?

_____

_____

Phase 3: Purchase and Conversion

This final phase involves new customers at the brink of making a purchase. You can facilitate this faster by offering first-time customer discount codes, limited-time offers, promotions where the customer purchases one service/ product and receives another free or at a discount, free trials, and loyalty programs, all of which can all help new customers complete the cycle and make a purchase.

What new customer incentives can you create?

_____

_____

Customer acquisition strategies will cost money (or time) to implement. One of the important business metrics you want to know is what it actually costs you to acquire a new customer. That is referred to as customer acquisition cost (or CAC, for short)

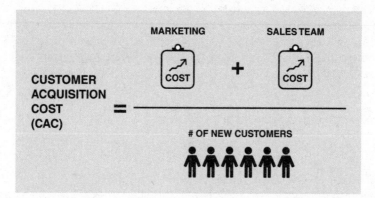

"Every business model involves some degree of customer churn" (Masterclass, 2022). That's technically what it's called, but the word "churn" always paints this gross milk visual for me, so I call it the customer burn rate. Simply defined, the customer burn rate is the amount of customers that drop off. In any business, you always need to be focused on increasing the total number of new customers to replace the old ones who have moved on. This is why an efficient customer acquisition process is important in predicting the long-term success and sustainability of a business.

Growth #2: Average Cart/Ticket— Increase the Average Transaction Amount That Your Customer Spends

Finding more customers isn't the only way to bring in more revenue. One of the best ways (and least expensive) is to bring in more income by increasing your average order.

Most commonly, the term "average ticket" is used in service-based businesses, and the term "average cart" is used in product-based, e-commerce, or online businesses. But they are one and the same.

Average cart, average ticket, average order value (AOV) are all terms used for the average amount your customers spend when they buy from you.

Understanding how to increase your AOV will increase your sales revenue, bringing in more revenue in a shorter period of time; will help offset your customer acquisition costs and recover that cost; and will increase the lifetime value of your customers (customer lifetime value: CLV).

Here are five ways to increase yours:

1. **Implement upselling and cross-selling:**

     Offering complementary products or services to your customers. This can be as simple as training your team to mention which items pair well with another or if you're online, cross-promote in your product descriptions. Make it clear in your messaging that your items gain more value when paired with other products, or these products are most commonly purchased with these products, all good ways to cross-promote.

     Upselling and cross-selling use the same skill set but are different.

     Upselling is upgrading the product the customer was originally planning on buying. For instance, if a customer comes in to buy the smallest, least expensive coffee in your store, upselling would be a more expensive (better quality) or a larger coffee purchase.

Cross-selling is adding a separate product or service to a sale. An example of this would be if a customer goes into a store to buy a belt and the associate convinces them to buy a pair of shoes to make it an outfit.

2. **Buying threshold incentives:**

A common strategy that online and big corporations use to increase their AOV is to get customers to meet certain thresholds on spending. You can see this offered in "Spend $50 and receive free shipping." If an order surpasses a certain amount, you can provide free shipping, free samples with a certain dollar amount, spend X and receive a free gift card for your next visit, or purchase 10 months and get 2 free.

3. **Promotions:**

Urgency can create the need to add more items to cart. A few examples of different tried and true promotions are: offering discount codes with a 24- to 72-hour window, physical coupons to redeem during a specific time, discounted rates or prices for bulk purchases or pre-buying, buying discounts (get $25 off your next $100 purchase), BOGO (buy one, get one), a free gift card with purchase, VIP access or a ticket to an event.

4. **Loyalty programs:**

They are a powerful way to build up your brand and retain existing customers. One study found that loyalty programs increase average order value by almost 20% on average. Loyalty programs are great for getting people to add more to their orders, and they help increase customer retention. Setting up a points system, with member/client benefits that reward customers for their purchases, encourages customer loyalty and higher purchase value, can increase buying frequency with member specials and promotions, and promotes client retention.

5. **Customer Service:**

In today's world, customer service is an underutilized weapon for increasing sales. I can't tell you how many businesses I've worked with over the years that have had not just bad but terrible customer service. With the ever-growing distractions of digital marketing, it seems easy to ignore the basics.

Simply put, customer service is the support you offer your customers— before they buy, after they buy, and while they use your products or services. It helps them have an easier and more enjoyable experience.

Of course there are skills with delivering great customer service— listening, empathy, patience, problem-solving, and going above and beyond—but before we even get to those, it starts with communication. Answering the phone, returning emails promptly, responding to social media messages, or adding technology to help you do just that.

Studies have shown that adding a live chat feature to your website alone can increase sales 10 to 15% more per cart, according to Forrester. When your customers get their questions answered, it leads to greater potential for a sale, less loss to a competitor, and fewer abandoned items in your online cart.

Growth #3: Buying Frequency/ Purchase Frequency (PF)—Increase the Amount of Times in Which Your Clients Buy from You

"Purchase frequency is one of the core metrics every business should track. It directly affects your profitability and revenue since you are *six times* more likely to sell to *existing* customers than *new* ones" (Lahunou, 2022). And it is more than *five times* more expensive to acquire a *new* customer than it is to sell an *existing* one.

Having existing clients buy your services and your products throughout the year will increase the customer lifetime value (CLV).

"High or average purchase frequency means customer loyalty, while low rates show that people rarely return after the first purchase" (Lahunou, 2022).

Here are three ways to increase your PF:

1. **Practice personalized email marketing.**

   When you want to increase the number of customers who make repeat purchases, remember that email marketing is an effective strategy. A convenient and standard communication tool, personalized email messages help you connect with customers regarding their purchases, or any special offers or sales you have that may interest them. Simply including the customer's name in an email subject line can increase the chance that they open your message by 26%. And having more opened emails can lead to getting more sales. Also, remember to customize the email content and presentation based on each individual's purchase history.

2. **Distribute limited-time offers.**

You can affect customers' buying behavior by offering deals for a limited time. Consumers who get the opportunity to purchase at a lower price are more likely to bite and actually buy (because they know that the price may go up). Even if they hadn't planned to buy what you're offering, they may do so because it just seems like a good deal.

This kind of buying behavior can increase the frequency of purchases and positively impact your revenue. Don't use the limited-time offer ploy too often; consumers can get used to experiencing these good deals and avoid making purchases that don't come with discount codes or sales. Also, consider how a "discount" image might negatively affect the overall purchase rate and perceived value of your brand.

3. **Treat customers with a loyalty program.**

Loyal customers are the best kind to have. One of the key principles in the business world is that people do business with those who they know, like, and trust. Customers who already love your brand and trust the integrity of your service/product may buy frequently even without your offering a loyalty program.

"Sixty percent of loyal customers say they are ready to purchase from their favorite companies" (Lahunou, 2022). That's why a customer loyalty program could result in more top-line sales for your business. Such a program might include points that accumulate with every purchase, special discounts and offers, or other incentives such as exclusive early access to sales for loyalty members. The other massive piece of this is loyal customers don't just buy more, they refer more. And there is no better customer than one that comes from a word-of-mouth referral from an existing customer. Direct referrals decrease your customer acquisition cost, and you're more likely to retain that customer because although they don't know, like, and trust you just yet, they have 58% greater chance of becoming a loyal customer from the recommendation of a friend than if they came in from other marketing efforts.

Growth #4: Raise Your Prices

This is the one that most people go to when wanting to increase revenue—but is not always the best decision. You want to look into, and understand, the data before raising prices across the board. However, on the other side of that, I have found that entrepreneurs don't necessarily understand the financial side of their businesses. Understanding all the numbers associated with business accounting and finance takes a lot of work. So when you need to look at increasing what you charge for your goods or services, look beyond emotions and concentrate on the data. Your own business data and industry research can support or deter the idea of raising prices. And the data won't give you bad advice, such as the adage "Charge what you're worth," (which sets you up to fail).

Gross profit is the telling factor. Know and track this number for your business. Basically, your gross profit is the amount of money left over after you pay for the direct expenses of making and distributing the products or services you offer.

We've seen that product costs, shipping costs, labor costs, gas prices, and even housing prices can jump significantly in one year—some changes occur even faster, depending on the industry or sector you're in. Situations like this put severe pressure on the gross profit number, and you may want to consider looking into how external factors affect your gross profit now, if you haven't already.

But when you do take that serious look at raising prices, understand that doing so offers you a chance to reevaluate critical elements of your business.

First, you have an opportunity to focus on value as it relates to all the expenditures you make to run the business. Of course, you want to provide quality service or products, hire excellent employees, and provide healthy wages and other benefits for your staff. Determine whether each of these expenditures contributes to value or needs an adjustment.

Second, your examination gives you a chance to reconsider the relationship with needy (revenue-draining) customers. You may get a lot of interaction with such customers, but they sometimes take up more time and resources than the revenue they generate warrants. I understand that giving up sales revenue is difficult, but you need to figure out whether keeping a current relationship with the needy customers serves your profitability.

I'll tell you that pricing your products and services correctly and fairly may actually eliminate problem customers. The gross profit you lose with those customers is then replaced by business generated from other customers who don't drain your profits. That is, you retain more of what you make with less work (or hassle).

Third, your close examination helps you identify and document your direct costs so that you can accurately determine your gross profit and gross margin.

Performing this evaluation to decide whether you want, or need, or should raise prices is a beneficial exercise on its own. If you've not delved this deep, doing so can increase your business finance acumen and really clarify how the business is coming along.

Try out these steps for gathering data and reevaluating your business's profitability:

1. Pull a report showing your customers and their sales volumes from your point of sale (POS) system or other sales software.

2. Determine the gross profitability for each of your customers and re-sort the report to reflect a top-to-bottom order of profitability.

3. Take a look at the bottom 20% of customers as determined in Step 2. Calculate how much gross profit (total dollars) that these 20% represent for your company.

4. Now ask yourself these questions:

   o How could you increase your value and pricing structure to replace that bottom 20% with a higher profitability?

   o Do you have a premium product or service that you've been wanting to launch?

   o How could you increase the buying frequency of the top 80% of customers to make up revenue lost by letting go of less profitable customers?

   o How many new customers would you need to acquire—at better profit margins—to replace the bottom 20%?

Pareto's principle is an adage used in business that states roughly 80% of outcomes come from 20% of causes—or, extrapolating to this business case, 20% of your efforts with customers will produce 80% of your profitability.

Timing when to make pricing or customer changes depends on your type of business and its sales cycles. Reevaluating your pricing gives you the opportunity to pinpoint your values, identify your ideal customers, and set the correct price for the market and your bottom line.

When you focus on revenue growth in the real business world and apply the four growth principles outlined in this chapter, you'll notice the difference in your income. Add that benefit to the tax savings advantages and self-education that comes with business ownership, you can see why it's a *wealth habit* that cannot, and should not, be ignored.

CHAPTER 11

Become the Ritz-Carlton of Your Industry and Create Cult-Like Customers

It was the fall of 1999. I was just starting my first business, and construction was underway on the commercial building. I got a call one day at my office. It was a travel agent that I met at a local business networking meeting. He had an incredible deal, with only a couple of spots left—a trip to Paris.

I instinctively knew that this was probably the only opportunity I was going to be able to travel—in a long time.

Up to this point in my life, I had never traveled out of the country. In fact, being 19 years old myself, growing up with teenage parents, and my dad having his own business, I didn't travel much at all.

But something about the thought of Paris, and this incredible deal, seemed just too good to pass up.

I took a quick flight to Newark, hopped on a connecting flight to London, and then onto Paris.

Of course, the culture was rich and the city was magnificent—from the Champs-Élysées and the Louvre, to Notre-Dame, the Eiffel Tower, and Arc de Triomphe—everything felt like it was sketched right out of a movie.

But what made the biggest impression on me was dining at the Ritz Paris, coffee at the Prince de Gallas, and stopping for crepes at the Four Seasons. I had never seen anything like it. People who made you feel like royalty, and like family, at the same time. It was a lot for my 19-year-old brain to fully comprehend, but what I did know was that I wanted to make people feel like that in my business.

After 10 days in Paris, I flew home and got to work. It was just months after returning home that the construction was completed, and I was ready to take our very first customers.

I read every book I could find on customer service, culture, and creating experience. I read all about the Marriott brand, Starbucks, and the Ritz-Carlton. I attended customer service trainings, created educational classes for my staff, took them to seminars on creating an exceptional experience, and even held sales contests that had prizes such as trips to the Ritz-Carlton hotels so they too could receive the experience I so wanted our teams to create.

You can't have a business without customers. It's that simple. But to create cult-like customers, customers who become ambassadors for your brand and tell others about you—well that takes providing value *and* creating an experience that they'll never forget.

We covered how to acquire more customers and increase revenue, but there is a business principle I mentioned in the last chapter: Success in business is determined by one thing—your ability to acquire new customers—*and* retain them long term.

There is a customer service principle I learned early on in my business that I want to share with you: **If you make customer experience a priority, you make price irrelevant.**

We can accomplish that by focusing on these three things:

1. **Experience:**

    Focus on the customer service you provide and the experience each customer has. You do this by creating a culture for your customers that helps them engage with your business and, more importantly, refer you to others.

2. **People:**

    Putting service before sales is the only way your business will remain sustainable. Today, many business owners focus on analytics, reports, and rankings but forget there are real people behind the screens. Real people are buying your products and services—they are choosing to spend their hard-earned dollars on your products or services rather than someone else's—truly valuing people will put you ahead of many others in your industry.

3. **Retention:**

    How do you keep those customers coming back? You create a cult-like customer base. Without customers, you don't have a business, so your focus must be there. Don't fall out of alignment with why you are here and why you do what you do.

    Creating a company culture focused on customer service isn't easy, but it's one of the most valuable things you can do in your business.

Ritz-Carlton is globally known for their customer culture and focus on customer experience. The secret to Ritz's unparalleled customer service lies in its strict adherence to its 100-year-old "Gold Standards." Their culture is weaved into everything they do including their pledge to "provide the finest personal service and facilities for guests who will always enjoy a warm, relaxed, yet refined ambiance."

Oftentimes when people are asked what company has great customer experience, they say Apple. But when Steve Jobs was opening Apple stores in the early 2000s, he sent all his future store managers to the Ritz-Carlton hospitality training.

Apple stores' phenomenal success shows that borrowing practices from great companies outside of your industry can produce game-changing results.

When focusing on your customers and customer service standards, think C.A.R.E.

C – Create a Standard

You need a customer service standard that everyone will follow. Your entire team must be on the same page. Spend as much time as you can here because it will be the foundation of your business.

Think about all aspects of customer service. What value do you want to provide? How will you handle problems? What protocols do you have in place? Create a standard and get everyone on the same page. It eliminates the guesswork and ensures your customers are handled with care every single time.

Having a customer-focused culture stops the back-and-forth and empowers your team to handle problems as they happen.

A – Anticipate and Fulfill Guests' Needs

If you want raving customers—the type who can't stop talking about your business—you need to go beyond what they need. You must go beyond what your products or services provide.

Think about it. What do you know about your customers? What is their family like? What do they love to do? Where do they go? Having this information helps you provide more value. You can take that extra step and anticipate their needs; this way when they come to you, they are blown away and can't help but tell others.

Every customer wants to be seen. Whether that's with value-added services, a small reward, or acknowledgment. They want to know that you see them and care about them. This creates the value-added service they want and will keep coming back to get.

R – Reward and Acknowledge

Customers love rewards—it keeps them coming back. Rewards don't have to be anything crazy—it's best if you keep it simple.

The old-school way was providing loyalty programs and you can still do that. Offer rewards for referrals, frequent purchases, number of visits, certain order sizes, or length of time as a customer. Think about your current sales goals.

Do you need more clients? Reward referrals.

Do you want to increase average cart/ticket? Reward spending thresholds.

Do you want to increase buying frequency? Reward number of visits.

Rewarding your best customers is a lot cheaper, and better than most other marketing and customer acquisition strategies.

Acknowledging your customers can start as simple as birthday cards, a discount code, or free gifts on their birthday or with a larger business, you can have someone on your team whose role is solely focused on customer experience.

Acknowledgment doesn't have to cost a lot of money. A simple phone call for a birthday or anniversary, a sympathy card for a loved one's death, or a congrats card on a special occasion—little things for your customers can go a long way.

E – Exceed Expectations

Finally, go above and beyond what your customers expect. Don't over-promise and then not deliver. That creates disappointed customers and bad publicity. Instead, take them by surprise.

Rather than, "I'll get back to you in two hours" when you know you can't get back for 24 hours, set the expectation that a response will be returned within 48 hours. When you respond back sooner—it's a pleasant surprise.

It doesn't matter what the issue is, create a situation where you can exceed the expectation. And the best way to find out how to do that is by listening. Customer files, notes about conversations, and customer preferences are all ways that will set you up to exceed expectations. It's always good business to go above and beyond—and apply a system so you can be *consistent*.

Think C.A.R.E. to create cult-like customers—customers who keep coming back no matter what because your service is unmatched. Be the business that goes above and beyond so that customers can't help but talk about you.

Establishing customer service standards, ensuring that those standards and practices are used throughout your business, and engaging and empowering employees will help you create the ultimate customer experience.

And you may be thinking that's not that easy, but nothing worth it ever is.

In 2022, the main drivers for the richest Americans were stocks and private businesses. Private businesses have been a powerful engine of wealth for those at the very top. The top 1% own 57% of private companies, according to the Federal Reserve (Frank, 2022).

Small business is really key when you talk about the sources of their wealth, and a small business can level out the "wealth inequality" as it's available to everyone.

Not everyone has tens of thousands of dollars to start buying stocks or buy their first investment property—but anyone can start a business.

If you want to catapult yourself into the ranks of the wealthy, the most likely way to get there *by far* is through starting a business.

Look at the Forbes 400 list. There are a few investors there—like Warren Buffett—but the vast majority of people there either started businesses, or inherited money from their family who started businesses.

You may not have the goal to be on the Forbes 400 list. But the truth is, even average Americans who start "boring" businesses—such as gutter cleaning, pressure washing, landscaping, tree trimming, house cleaning, holiday decorating, laundry service, dog waste removal, auto repair shops, personal assisting, or carpet cleaning—will likely become wealthier than those who just focus on retirement investing alone.

Building a business is a powerful *wealth habit*. It's the engine that runs the American economy—and it's the engine that will run your personal economy—while leading you to the wealth you want and deserve.

WEALTH HABIT 4

Saving Your Way to Wealth

CHAPTER 12

It's Not How Much You Earn, It's How Much You Keep: How to Give as Little Money as Legally Possible to the IRS

"The amount of tax you pay ultimately depends on whether you are educated or uneducated about the system."

I'm known for being obsessed with giving as little of my money to the IRS as is humanly, *and legally,* possible.

Is this because I hate the IRS and taxes?

Well, who doesn't, but that's not the point.

The point is that the difference between a moderately successful entrepreneur and a truly wealthy entrepreneur is in how much attention they pay to keeping more of what they make—and taxes is one of those areas.

You can bring in tons of revenue and keep your expenses low so you make a profit. And you think, "I'm rich!" But guess what, you're not going to be if you're not smart about taxes.

Ignorance about taxes is one of the ways I see otherwise successful entrepreneurs bleed money out of their bottom line.

Next to bad debt, taxes can be another knife to the heart of your wealth.

How on earth did this whole thing start, and why don't we know more about it?

What follows is a quick look at history of taxation in the United States.

A Brief History

During the US Civil War, the first federal income tax was created in 1861 as a way to finance the war. Subsequently, in 1862, Congress passed the Internal Revenue Act, which created the Bureau of Internal Revenue (the modern-day IRS). Following the end of the Civil War, the income tax did not have substantial support and was repealed just 10 years later in 1872. Twenty or so years after that, the next stages in the changing history of federal income taxation began as follows:

- In 1894: Congress established an income tax rate of 2%, but it was later overturned by the Supreme Court.

- In February 1913, states ratified the Sixteenth Amendment to the Constitution, which granted Congress the power to tax personal income. This new system collected income tax at the source, as it is still done today, where taxes are initially withheld from a person's paycheck before the income reaches the recipient.

- In 1914: The Bureau of Internal Revenue released the first income tax form (Form 1040). Although it's had modifications almost every year since 1914, Form 1040 is still the main income tax form used today.

- By 1915: Members of Congress and the public voiced concerns about the complexity of the income tax form, stating the difficulty of preparing and filing returns.

- In 1916: The Revenue Act (of 1916) initiated the practice of adjusting tax rates and income scales. Originally, income tax was 1% for the lowest income bracket (a yearly income up to $20,000) and 7% for the top income bracket (a yearly income over $500,000).

Historical Highest Marginal Income Tax Rates

Year	Top Marginal Rate	Year	Top Marginal Rate	Year	Top Marginal Rate	Year	Top Marginal Rate
1913	7.00%	1948	82.13%	1983	50.00%	2018	37.00%
1914	7.00%	1949	82.13%	1984	50.00%	2019	37.00%
1915	7.00%	1950	84.36%	1985	50.00%	2020	37.00%
1916	15.00%	1951	91.00%	1986	50.00%	2021	37.00%
1917	67.00%	1952	92.00%	1987	38.50%	2022	37.00%
1918	77.00%	1953	92.00%	1988	28.00%		
1919	73.00%	1954	91.00%	1989	28.00%		
1920	73.00%	1955	91.00%	1990	28.00%		
1921	73.00%	1956	91.00%	1991	31.00%		
1922	58.00%	1957	91.00%	1992	31.00%		
1923	43.50%	1958	91.00%	1993	39.60%		
1924	46.00%	1959	91.00%	1994	39.60%		
1925	25.00%	1960	91.00%	1995	39.60%		
1926	25.00%	1961	91.00%	1996	39.60%		
1927	25.00%	1962	91.00%	1997	39.60%		
1928	25.00%	1963	91.00%	1998	39.60%		
1929	24.00%	1964	77.00%	1999	39.60%		
1930	25.00%	1965	70.00%	2000	39.60%		
1931	25.00%	1966	70.00%	2001	39.10%		
1932	63.00%	1967	70.00%	2002	38.60%		
1933	63.00%	1968	75.25%	2003	35.00%		
1934	63.00%	1969	77.00%	2004	35.00%		
1935	63.00%	1970	71.75%	2005	35.00%		
1936	79.00%	1971	79.00%	2006	35.00%		
1937	79.00%	1972	70.00%	2007	35.00%		
1938	79.00%	1973	70.00%	2008	35.00%		
1939	79.00%	1974	70.00%	2009	35.00%		
1940	81.00%	1975	70.00%	2010	35.00%		
1941	81.00%	1976	70.00%	2011	35.00%		
1942	88.00%	1977	70.00%	2012	35.00%		
1943	88.00%	1978	70.00%	2013	39.60%		
1944	94.00%	1979	70.00%	2014	39.60%		
1945	94.00%	1980	70.00%	2015	39.60%		
1946	86.45%	1981	69.13%	2016	39.60%		
1947	86.45%	1982	50.00%	2017	39.60%		

Notes: This table contains a number of simplifications and ignores a number of factors, such as the amount of income or types of income subject to the top rates, or the value of standard and itemized deductions.

Sources: IRS Revenue Procedures, various years. Also, Eugene Steuerle, The Urban Institute; Joseph Pechman, *Federal Tax Policy*; Joint Committee on Taxation, Summary of Conference Agreement on the Jobs and Growth Tax Relief Reconciliation Act of 2003, JCX-54-03, May 22, 2003.

Provided by Tax Policy Center

Tax policies, along with many other government policies, present a slippery slope. The idea that began as a means to fund a war has become a part of everyday lives. The tax code is ever changing and has been amended or revised over 4,000 times (an estimate) in just the past 10 years. In 1913, you could print the US Tax Code on a single page; today, it would span up to 6,871 pages and contains more than 4.12 million words. An average adult would need almost two weeks to read it!

Taxes Are Personal

The reason the topic is important for me to teach and help you understand is because the average American, or even business owner, doesn't have the resources to hire a full-time tax strategist or controller. Nor do they have the time to research and digest all of those pages of the IRS code, but massive corporations do.

Corporations have the time and money to not only squeeze every deduction and loophole, but they have the power to leverage tax law and create exemptions through hiring lobbyists to get into the pocket of our lawmakers.

What most business owners fail to acknowledge is that we are able to use all of those same deductions and reduce our own taxes but more often than not, we aren't even aware they exist.

I could write an entire book about taxes, but this is not a tax planning book. My goal is to simply help explain the rules in super plain English and break down complex topics to make them super simple to understand. Because the more you know about taxes, the more you understand how they apply to you and your business, which will result in more money you can save, resulting in greater wealth.

These principles do not take the place of the important role a tax strategist and a tax preparer have in your business. The tax code and tax laws change constantly, and every single person's situation is uniquely different.

However, my goal is to help educate you on this topic so you can ask the proper questions and make the intelligent decisions on your tax planning strategy.

The More You Know, the Less You End Up Paying

If you're not working with someone who is savvy and constantly educating themselves on tax code for businesses specifically, it will end up costing you a lot of money.

Americans pay many types of taxes. They all fall into two tax categories: direct and indirect. Direct taxes include income taxes, property taxes, capital gains taxes, and estate taxes. Indirect tax is the tax levied on the consumption of goods and services such as sales tax, gas tax, cigarette and alcohol tax, and value added tax (VAT).

But because of how the tax system is set up, the most amount of tax you will ever pay is on your earned income—your job, your W2.

The quicker you can take earned money and invest it to create passive or portfolio income—investments or rental properties—the less tax you will pay and the more you get to keep in your pocket.

There are three more basics they never taught us in high school (or in college for that matter) and that you need to be aware of:

1. **How Deductions (aka Write-Offs) Work**
2. **Why Proper Bookkeeping Means Everything to Your Tax Bill**
3. **The Red Flags and Audits No One Wants**

Let's go through each of these.

1. How Deductions (aka Write-Offs) Work

A tax deduction reduces your taxable income and, consequently, the amount of taxes you owe.

The higher your tax bracket (the percentage of the income you owe in taxes), the more beneficial a tax deduction is.

For example, if you're in the 35% bracket a $1,000 deduction saves you $350. But if you're in the 15% bracket, it only saves you $150.

So let's unpack this.

Business write-offs are tax deductions. You'll hear the terms interchanged, but it relates to purchases that are made and are essential to running a business.

These expenses are subtracted from revenue to figure out total taxable income for a company. The more write-offs, the lower the taxable income—reducing the amount of tax owed.

Self-employed individuals incur many expenses when building a business, and the IRS allows you to write-off those expenses as they are needed for the business to generate income. For these expenses to qualify as deductions, they must be "ordinary and necessary" in the business. You can subtract a dollar from your taxable business income for every dollar you spend when the expenses are fully deductible.

What Does "Ordinary and Necessary" Mean?

The IRS states that an ordinary expense is one that is common and accepted in your industry. A necessary expense is one that is helpful and appropriate for your trade or business.

Ordinary and necessary business expenses can include everything from office supplies to liability insurance and work boots to computers.

Should you ever be audited, "ordinary and necessary" is a category the IRS will look at when determining your eligibility for deductions. It would be your responsibility to prove entries, deductions, and statements made on your tax returns—this is considered the burden of proof.

Remember: Should you ever be audited, you must be able to prove (substantiate) certain elements of expenses to deduct them.

The Six Ps of a Proper Tax Deduction:

Place – where you purchased the item;

Point in time – the date when you purchased the item;

Purchase amount – total purchase amount for expenditure;

Present documentation – the physical or digital version receipt;

Person – who the expense was with (for meals, meetings, events);

Purpose – the reason for the purchase.

Most receipts automatically have the first three—place, date, amount—but to make deductions legit (should you get audited) specifically for things such as meals and entertainment, you need purpose and person for your deduction to be valid.

My friend Pat is a tax attorney, and among his many stories is one on this exact topic.

Pat had a client in the middle of a nasty audit, which resulted in having to go to tax court (somewhere we never want to be). In preparation for court they reviewed a batch of receipts to see if there was enough supporting documentation to substantiate the deductions. While reviewing, he noticed that they were not marked appropriately which could have resulted in a negative outcome in tax court. Having appropriate documentation is critical and not knowing this type of information can end up costing you a *lot* of money.

Commonly Deducted Expenses

Following is a list of the most common, fully deductible business expenses that are pretty standard regardless of the business you're in:

Accounting fees

Advertising and marketing

Bank charges

Business entertainment

Business insurance

Commissions and sales costs

Consulting expenses

Continuing professional education costs

Contract labor costs

Credit and collection fees

Delivery charges

Dues and subscriptions

Electricity

Employee benefit programs

Equipment rentals

Insurance

Interest paid

Internet subscriptions, domain names, web hosting

Legal fees

Licenses

Maintenance and repairs

Office furniture

Office supplies

Pension and profit-sharing plans

Postage

Printing and copying expenses

Rent

Salaries, wages, other compensation

Security

Software

Taxes

Telephone

Travel

Worker's compensation costs

Nondeductible Business Expenses

Some business costs are directly related to operating a business, but are not deductible under any circumstances. Things such as:

- Illegal payments (bribes or kickbacks)
- Fines and penalties
- Lobbying expenses or political contributions
- Dues and membership fees you might pay for social clubs unrelated to the type of business

Check out Publication 535, Business Expenses on the IRS website (**www.irs.gov**) for more in-depth information on non-deductible expenses.

Now That You're Self-Employed, Meet Your Nemesis: Mr. Self-Employment Tax

Self-employment tax refers to the Medicare and Social Security taxes self-employed people must pay. This includes freelancers, independent contractors, and small business owners.

The current self-employment tax rate is 15.3%—which includes 12.4% for Social Security and 2.9% for Medicare—and an additional 0.9% Medicare tax rate applies if your net income from self-employment exceeds $250,000 for married filing jointly and $200,000 if filing single.

Employers and employees share the self-employment tax, and each pays 7.65%. People who are fully self-employed, or own a business, have to pay the total 15.3% themselves. (This is depending on how your business is structured. See Chapter 9 for more on how to reduce this.)

How to Avoid the Double Tax: Let's Break It Down

We covered a lot of this in the Chapter 9 under the Business Structure section, so go back and review if you need a refresher on the terms.

The reason I needed to add this here is because of the tax implications and how it applies to the small business owner.

Corporations are always going to pay the most amount of tax—that's why they are called the double taxation corporation. They get nailed with corporate tax *and* personal tax—double tax.

However, an S corporation doesn't have to pay corporate taxes and only pays self-employment tax on its wages.

For example, let's say you currently make $100,000 in your business (as a sole proprietor). If you were operating as a sole proprietor or LLC that entire $100,000 profit (sole prop) is subject to self-employment tax, currently 15.3%, resulting in $15,300 for just that tax.

So let's say you elect to file as an S corporation and pay yourself a salary that's usual and customary in your industry, $40,000. Your *salary* is subject to the 15.3% self-employment tax resulting in $6,120 as your SETax. But the remaining $60,000 would not be subject to self-employment tax. This one shift in your business structure just saved over $9,000 in taxes!

There's a lot to keep track of when it comes to your taxes. That's why proper bookkeeping is critical. And why bookkeeping is one of the most important things you need to have in your business because without it you won't be able to take many of the deductions I've been talking about in the book! This results in you leaving thousands of dollars on the table and paying far more taxes than you need.

2. Why Proper Bookkeeping Means Everything to Your Tax Bill

Proper bookkeeping is the lifeblood of your business. It's essential for five reasons:

1. It makes your deductions more defensible to the IRS, and therefore supports you in taking more deductions.
2. It enables you to keep your finger on the pulse of your business and catch problem areas before they spiral out of control.
3. It allows you to prevent cash flow disasters that could tank your business.
4. It is essential for selling your business, attracting investments, or bringing on a partner.
5. It can help you spot embezzlement or other issues in your business—like careless waste by employees.

As someone who has been embezzled by employees more than once over the last 25 years, I can't stress how important this last point is. *Don't* think, "It can't happen to me." Even when you have a consistent handle on your finances, it can happen, but if you don't understand your numbers, or aren't monitoring them regularly, it's even easier for issues to arrive.

Turn your fear around knowing your numbers into something fun.

What I'm going to share with you is a little thing I've done, almost without fail, for more than 20 years.

Knowing your numbers and developing your financial acumen doesn't have to be boring and dreadful. It can be sexy, fun, and something you look forward to doing. (*And even if you don't have a business you can do this with your personal financial statements!*)

Hold a State of the Union Meeting

It's human nature to ignore that which we don't understand or enjoy.

Holding a state of the union meeting is something I started doing decades ago, and it radically changed my business and my personal wealth.

Keeping up to date and having a current financial picture of your finances is essential—for your business *and* your personal finances. It helps you make informed decisions that have the potential to make a big impact on your business, your growth, and your bottom line. It helps you know what's working, what you're spending too much on, and in what areas you can cut expenses.

Business at its core is all about numbers, and those numbers are telling you a story. If you want to be in business or build lasting personal wealth, you need to understand that financial story.

Take the time to invest in the skills everyone needs to build lasting wealth.

And if you find financial information intimidating or scary, you are not alone. Most of the entrepreneurs I work with used to avoid their numbers like the plague. But once they started learning it and doing the state of the union meeting, they realized it wasn't so scary—it was something to look forward to. And the only way to learn anything new is to start doing it!

The bottom line here is that you deserve better. You deserve to become wealthy, and when you know your numbers it helps you get there more quickly. Investing in this knowledge will build unshakable confidence in your business and your personal finances.

There are four steps to conducting your very own state of the union meeting:

1. Schedule a meeting with yourself once a month. This should ideally be by the 10th, but no later than the 15th of the month (so you have ample time for your bookkeeper to reconcile your bank accounts for the month prior).

2. Prepare and print your three critical business financial statements (or four, if you have investors) as well as your bank reconciliations. (If you don't yet have a business, you would run the financial reports, any expenses—credit card statements, bills, and loan payments of any kind—for your personal accounts.)

3. Prepare and print your point-of-sale (POS) and/or customer relationship management (CRM) reports (the system or software you process and keep track of sales) as well as any corresponding sales, customer, or employee data. The goal is to get all of the reports needed in order to get a full snapshot of your business.

4. The best part. My favorite part. Go to a restaurant, a resort, a coffee shop, or grab a glass of wine with a view and take everything with you—get out of the office. Make this a recurring two-hour appointment with yourself every month. Turn the phone on silent and flip it upside down. Review all the data and start to listen to what the numbers are telling you.

Pro tip: This is also a great time to record minutes in your corporate book.

Most states require S corporations to keep meeting minutes. Depending on what state you live in, you will likely be required to hold regular shareholder meetings and keep minutes of such meetings. If you are ever sued or become part of a lawsuit, any good business attorney is going to ask to see your corporate book in an effort to discredit your business and pierce the veil of any corporation or LLC you may have.

Piercing the Veil

Piercing the corporate veil (going around the business entity designed to protect you and going after the business owner themselves) is what every attorney will try to do and what every business owner needs to protect against. If they are successful in this, it will open you up to personal liability, and the court can hold you—and any other owners or shareholders—liable for the corporation's action or debts.

My friend Cody is a business attorney and a pit bull litigator. He's the guy you want protecting you, but the guy you don't want to be against in court. He has successfully broken through LLCs and corporations on countless occasions and was able to go after the owners personally.

Cody and I were talking about a case in which the corporate veil was pierced successfully because the owner was sloppy with finances.

The business owner had been in business for nearly 20 years. His corporation agreed to services for a customer, a construction company. After beginning work on the project, the corporation abandoned the work. The construction company obtained a $400,000 judgment against the corporation for breach of contract but was unable to collect on the judgment. The construction company then filed a new action seeking to pierce the veil of the corporation and recover personally from the owner.

The courts can work around that liability protection "if the corporation is undercapitalized, if it lacks separate books, if its finances are not kept separate from individual finances or individual obligations are paid by the corporation, if the corporation is used to promote fraud or illegality, or if corporate formalities are not followed" (Tidgren, 2018) (this is why I stress the importance of separate accounts and finances).

In this case, the court went through each formality and account one by one. It found insufficient evidence that could establish the business as undercapitalized or purposely underfunded by the defendant; the business operated for 20 years. They found no fraud occurred because the owner and the corporation were known as legitimate. But there was evidence that showed the owner did not maintain a *separate entity* from the businesses, and therefore, the court ruling was that the corporate veil should be pierced.

Unfortunately, although the business owner kept a separate bank account for the business, he also commingled its funds with personal finances. The owner used the accounts interchangeably for transactions of the corporation in question as well as his other businesses.

The defendant did not adequately track the business' books, nor did he follow required corporate formalities. He could not produce a record of bylaws, corporate minutes, or a shareholder ledger, nor documentation of a shareholder meeting for the corporation.

The owner did file biennial reports after 2000, but the reports were often filed after the deadline. As a result, the corporation was administratively reinstated three times. Neglecting to follow such corporate formalities did not help the owner's case and added weight to the other factors.

The case details clearly show that corporate protections apply only to businesses that follow the applicable laws. Remember that protecting the owner's liability requires that business and personal finances (including specific books for all entities) remain separate. The law is clear on this issue. Here is the bottom-line: Adhere to the formalities of owning a corporation, including filing the required reports, holding the right meetings, and keeping proper books (shareholder, financial, and otherwise) accurate and up to date. In general, LLCs require fewer formalities. In this case, however, the results would likely have been the same even if the corporation were an LLC. Never commingle business and personal expenses; the quickest way to lose liability protection is to pay personal expenses out of business accounts and fail to keep separate books. If this happens, shareholders' personal assets (your house, car, personal savings) may be exposed to liability for the corporation's debts.

Having to keep meeting minutes may seem like a trivial thing, particularly for smaller S corporations, but failure to keep meeting minutes as governed by your state's laws can attract serious consequences.

LLCs may not be required to keep corporate minutes, but annual reports and other documentation can be required depending on your state. Use your State of the Union Meeting to hold such review, and recorded minutes will keep you compliant and serve as protection should you ever be exposed to a lawsuit. You can find reasonable books for LLC or corporations on Amazon. I have my favorites tagged on: **www.candyvalentino.com/shop**.

Business Always Boils Down to Numbers and Data

Keep on top of your numbers yourself, but remember you don't actually have to do the grunt work of the data entry and bookkeeping. Bookkeeping is a perfect example of something you should outsource to pros to free up more of your time.

But unless you are at scale and have extensive systems in place, the one role you never want to outsource is "being on top of the numbers." It's an easy way to be removed from your business while letting expenses get out of control or have an issue with theft or embezzlement. Embezzlers, thieves, and dishonest people in general, *love* business owners who ignore their numbers and outsource the effort of keeping the bird's-eye view of the business.

A bookkeeper is distinct from a tax strategist and/or tax preparer.

For example, a tax strategist first told me about the "Augusta Rule," which allows me to rent my own home to my business, tax free. And Section 179 is a strategy for deducting a large portion of vehicles, including some luxury SUVs.

Much different than a tax preparer, having a tax advisor and strategist will pay for itself many times over.

What's the difference? If you're getting your taxes prepared, you're operating in a reactive state *after* your business year is over. If you're not proactively planning your taxes with monthly, quarterly, or semi-annual meetings, you're going to miss out on using massive tax reduction strategies and put hundreds, thousands, or even hundreds of thousands of dollars into the IRS's pockets, instead of yours.

Hiring someone who focuses on tax strategy and keeps up to date on business taxes is one of the most important investments you can make. Go to **www.candyvalentino.com** for help with business tax strategy.

3. The Red Flags and Audits No One Wants

One of the most common misconceptions about audits is how often they are performed and *your* chances of getting that dreaded letter from the IRS. So many people worry about the possibility of facing an audit that they leave thousands of dollars on the table and overpay the IRS.

Yet in 2021, the IRS audited less than half of 1% of tax returns—0.4% of all returns were audited.

This percentage does go up as you earn more money; however, the audit rate was still less than 1% for those who earned up to $1 million in income.

On average, 1 to 2% of businesses get audited each year (it can be slightly higher or lower, depending on the amount of your return). My point is the chance of an audit for most people in any given year is low. However, if you're in business for 10 to 20 years, or a high wage earner, the cumulative chance of being audited is obviously higher.

The IRS uses a computer system called the Discriminant Inventory Function, or DIF to monitor tax returns.

One of the top ways to trigger an audit is to have a disproportionate number of contractors (issued 1099s) versus employees (issued W-2s). Of course, this may be the legitimate reality for your business, and if so, you can defend it.

However, if you're inclined to be "loose" about whom you classify as a contractor to avoid payroll taxes, don't. The last thing you want is to trigger an audit for reasons you can't defend. Let's get clear on the top distinctions between a contractor and an employee.

While the determination often relies on a mix of factors—and no single aspect may be decisive—some of the main factors that suggest your worker is an employee, not a contractor, include:

1. You exercise behavioral control over the worker. This means you generally tell them not just what to do ("Please design a logo for me") but also how, when, and where to do it ("Please design a logo for me, and you must use this specific set of steps, with these specific tools, and you must do it at this desk in our office between these specific hours.").

2. You exercise financial control over the worker. You are their main source of income, and you prevent them (via noncompete clauses) from seeking out similar work in your industry. You ask for (and guarantee) a specific number of hours of work per week.

3. Your arrangement has other elements that make it seem like an employment relationship: health benefits, paid vacation or sick days, retirement benefits. The work is open-ended and expected to endure past specific projects. The worker is performing a central function of your business. For example, you are a law firm, and the worker is working directly with your firm's clients, under your firm's banner and brand.

Deductions the IRS Looks at a Little Closer

Even though the IRS only audited 0.4% of income tax returns in 2021, many people live in fear of a letter from the IRS questioning items on their return. Because of the possibility of facing an IRS audit, many people hesitate to claim all the tax breaks they are entitled to claim, and when they do this, they are leaving their money on the table (U.S. News and World Report, 2022).

Yes, you should deduct all legitimate expenses, but the IRS's Big Brother software keeps a keen eye for auditing businesses with large deductions.

Keep meticulous records for every expense related to these:

Home office: One of the most common tax deductions that people leave on the table is the home office deduction.

You can deduct your actual expenses, including a portion of your mortgage interest, homeowners or renters insurance, and utilities—gas, electric, garbage, Internet, and so on—based on the area of your home you use as an office. Keep records of all of those expenses. The IRS has been known to monitor these *closely*. You don't ever want to take deductions that aren't legitimate.

The alternative is the simplified option: $5 per square foot of your home office, up to 300 square feet, for a maximum deduction of $1,500.

Real-life example: Let's say you have a 3000 sq ft house and a 300 sq ft office (10% of the total square footage). You would get to deduct 10% of all related bills which could keep anywhere from $1,500 to $2,500 in your pocket—and not in Uncle Sam's.

It is important you work with an educated tax professional who understands business taxes. This used to be a common red flag that CPAs advised against, but in the modern era of everyone truly working from home, it can be a very real and valid deduction for business owners.

To qualify, you must use part of your home "regularly and exclusively" for business. It doesn't need to be in a separate room, but it has to be a space that isn't used for anything but your office.

Meals and entertainment: Gone are the days of taking clients to strip clubs because in 2018, the government cracked down on this abuse and deducting entertainment became entirely disallowed. However, in 2022, you can deduct 100% of meals—food and beverages—provided by a restaurant. The 100% deduction is set to expire on December 31, 2022, and go back to the pre-pandemic amount of 50%. The IRS believes deductions for business meals are particularly prone to misuse, so you must document these deductions meticulously using the Six Ps of a Proper Deduction from earlier in the chapter and document each with purpose and person (the two that will not be included on a receipt).

Lots of cash transactions or large cash transactions: If you're in a cash-based business, cash transactions are inevitable—but keep meticulous records. And if you've got a suitcase of hundreds and want to buy something with it that you then deduct—it's probably better to deposit it in the bank first and use a check!

IRS auditors keep a keen eye on businesses who receive cash payments— grocery stores, restaurants, mobile food trucks, auto dealers and repair shops, salons and spas, landscapers, and gas stations. They are particularly interested in underreported income, and improper accounting for COGS (cost of goods sold). If you are in one of these businesses, be extra careful.

And remember that any cash transaction over $10,000 made at a bank, car dealership, trade, or business is required to be reported to the IRS by using Form 8300. You'll want to avoid that at all costs.

Amended returns: The IRS casts a more suspicious eye on amended returns (as they indicate you weren't very careful with your bookkeeping), late returns and late payroll taxes (which indicate disorganization), and paper returns (as they are much more prone to mistakes). If the amount you're going to gain from the amendment is trivial, it's probably best to avoid the extra risk. And these days, there's no reason to file a paper return!

Charitable donations: We all love great charities who do great work in the world. And donating to charitable causes meaningful to you is an important wealth habit. However, if you're more generous than normal with your business donations, the IRS can get skeptical. Make sure you get an acknowledgment letter from the 501c3 for any cash donations or even substantial in-kind (non-cash) donations. Keep those records safe should you ever need them.

Business losses: You can deduct a lot of expenses from your business. However, the IRS wants to make sure you did not set up a business just for the purpose of taking deductions. If you show net losses year after year, or barely any profit at a break-even point, this could raise concern and trigger an audit. The general rule of thumb is that reporting a loss more than two out of five years is a red flag. If the loss isn't that big, you might want to consider foregoing some deductions and report a small profit. You'll also forgo the carry-forward loss for next year, but you'll thereby avoid this big audit red flag.

Not reporting stock trades: Unless the investments are in a tax-deferred account, trades are taxable when you sell the shares. Most firms will send you a 1099B, and you need to report the capital gains and losses.

Crypto: The IRS increasingly sees cryptocurrency as a hotspot for tax avoidance. If you make any cryptocurrency trades, sales, or expenditures, be sure to fill out Form 8949, Sales and Other Dispositions of Capital Assets. Unfortunately, even if you use a cryptocurrency to buy something, it's considered a taxable event, subject to capital gains/losses. Figuring out the cost basis of every sale across multiple platforms you may use can be tricky. Fortunately, there are many software programs that can calculate and fill out your crypto taxes easily.

Math and general errors: If you're using lots of big round numbers, you're likely "guesstimating" your numbers, and the IRS can get skeptical. Always make sure you double-check for simple errors such as math mistakes, rounding up numbers, your name on the wrong line, an error in your Social Security number. Remember to always report all of your income. Income from a 1099 or W-2 is going to be reported to the IRS. They can easily check your income reported from employers, banks, and brokers against your tax returns. Always check the accuracy and work with a pro.

Business use of personal car: If you're doing this, you will need to document miles and business purpose of every single business ride. You can use the standard mileage rate or the actual expense rate to determine the amount you can deduct. If you have a car used *only* for business purposes, you may be able to deduct its entire cost. Topic No. 510 at **irs.gov** has more details.

Business use of personal cell phone: You need to document the *percentage* of cell phone use that is business, which means you literally need to track the minutes of every call, business and personal, to come up with a percentage. Again, who has time for that? It's far easier to have a separate phone for business than it is to try and keep track of the percentage you use your personal phone for business.

S corp salary: If you're an S corp, you need to pay yourself a "reasonable salary" for your field. If you give yourself an unusually low salary to avoid Social Security or other taxes, the IRS will notice, and this behavior will certainly increase your risk for an audit.

Out of the ordinary activity: If you've been filing your business returns for some time and have a large increase in deductions all of a sudden, it could look suspish. If you've suddenly discovered massive new categories of deductions, and you want to prioritize avoiding the headache of an audit, it's probably wise to ramp them up over a few years rather than jump wildly from one year to the next. But if they are legit deductions and it makes sense for you to reduce your taxable income now and you can substantiate the deduction, just make sure you can support the write-off. The IRS is going to compare your deductions to others in your similar income tax bracket and business industry/type. Having properly maintained books is crucial to your business should you ever have to prove legitimate deductions.

My point is this: Don't leave money on the table when it comes to taking the deductions. Take the ones you can legally take. Have clear records, keep all supporting documentation, and work with a tax strategist pro. No one wants to pay an arm and a leg to have their taxes done, but no one wants to pay any more in taxes than they're truly supposed to. And one corner you do *not* want to cut is trying to save a few bucks and file your taxes on your own.

Remember that every dollar you deduct from your taxable income is a dollar you can use to keep investing, hire more staff, develop new products and services, and continue to build your business. That's why reducing your taxes and keeping more of the money you make is a *wealth habit* that cannot be ignored.

CHAPTER 13

Three Secret Tax Strategies That Sound Illegal (But Are Actually Totally Legal!)

I'm a law-abiding citizen.

I also love using perfectly legal tax strategies and loopholes that make me think, "How the #&$! is this legal?!"

Hey, I don't make the rules. The IRS does. But if they're going to make rules that sound too good to be true—but are in fact true—you bet I'm going to take advantage of them. And you can too!

I get that these tax secrets—like how to write off luxury SUVs or vacation homes—aren't for everyone, if you're just starting your business. They're more helpful for people who have already advanced in their business earnings.

But if you follow the other steps in this book and build your business right, they could be relevant for you soon.

Not only can these tax secrets excite you by showing you what's possible, they also teach an important lesson: The tax code is written to help business owners and rich people.

You may think, "That's not fair!" but it's a good reason to become a business owner and start building the *wealth habits* so you can make them work for you too.

Please note, all of these depend on you owning a business. And, as always, I'm not a tax professional. I'm a self-made businesswoman who has done my research (insane amounts of research) and has made use of these strategies, over and over. But you should always consult your own tax professional before using any of these secrets yourself. Okay, now that the legal stuff is out of the way for the lawyers, let's dive in.

1. A Tax-Deduction in the Playroom: Hire Your Kids for $12,000 per Year Each Tax-Deductible for You, Tax-Free for Them

My client Caroline has three kids: a 9-year-old girl and 11- and 13-year-old boys. She was taking the current child tax credit of $2,000 per child, a tax break of $6,000 per year.

Caroline ran a small business selling mugs, t-shirts, and other items with funny and sarcastic sayings and jokes printed on them. She was selling her merchandise on Amazon, in her own Shopify store, and with other online retail outlets.

I asked her, "Is there a reason you don't have your kids on payroll?"

Caroline said, "What do you mean? I've never heard of that!"

Her kids were already working inside the business, doing odd jobs. The nine-year-old was more mature (as girls tend to be at that age—hey, just sayin'!) ;) So mom gave her more "prestigious" jobs, such as sorting inventory when it came in and stuffing and labeling packages.

The boys did "heavier" work like packing the larger boxes that went to the retailers, cleaning up around the office, and sweeping the sidewalks outside.

At my suggestion, Caroline put her three kids on payroll, each with a job description, and she paid them $1,000 a month. This was a $36,000 tax deduction for her business. (If it's less than $12,000 per year of income each, your children don't have to pay taxes on it.)

But much more important than a tax deduction were all the things her kids were learning. Something I call the **50/25/25 rule**.

Caroline loved this concept and made the following deal with her kids: Half of what they earned, 50%, they put into saving/investing, via a custodial Roth IRA she set up for them. This alone was enough to set them up for success.

Investing $500 a month can result in close to $200,000 dollars in their Roth IRA (depending on when it was started) at 18 years old—giving a return of just 7%,which is lower than the historical growth rates of the stock market. And even if there isn't another penny added to the account, that same amount will turn into *millions* at age 65 when it's time to retire. That's the power of compounding interest. It's actionable steps like these that not only set your kids up for financial success, but it teaches them the skills and the importance of financial literacy and investing!

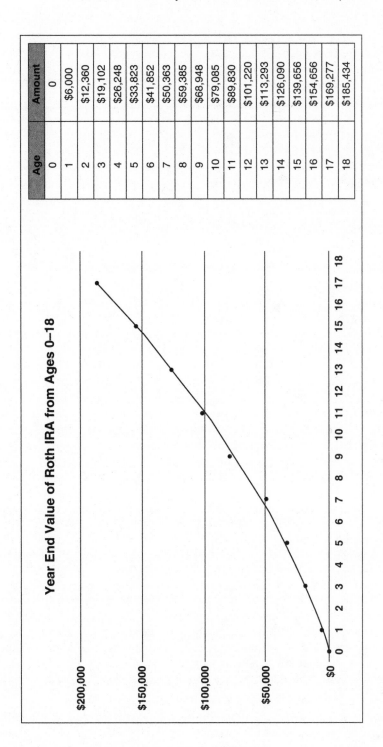

Age	Amount
0	0
1	$6,000
2	$12,360
3	$19,102
4	$26,248
5	$33,823
6	$41,852
7	$50,363
8	$59,385
9	$68,948
10	$79,085
11	$89,830
12	$101,220
13	$113,293
14	$126,090
15	$139,656
16	$154,656
17	$169,277
18	$185,434

Year End Value of Roth IRA from Ages 0–18

Over time, this approach also shows them even more ways to build wealth. Like how buying stock in the companies that make the cool things they want is much better than buying those cool things.

Show your kids this: The original iPhone retailed for $499–$599 based on the amount of storage on June 29, 2007. If you would have invested in Apple stock, instead of buying the iPhone, because of the stock splits it went through it would now be worth $510,720. A half a million bucks! Whereas the first iPhone is now an expensive paperweight at best.

They can have the same results investing in the companies that make whatever latest gizmo they want.

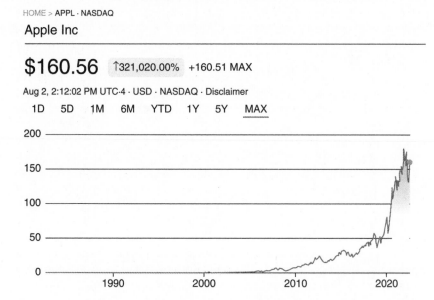

HOME > APPL · NASDAQ

Apple Inc

$160.56 ↑321,020.00% +160.51 MAX

Aug 2, 2:12:02 PM UTC-4 · USD · NASDAQ · Disclaimer

1D   5D   1M   6M   YTD   1Y   5Y   MAX

Long before iPhones, I got my own education in this type of thinking. Every year for my birthday, my great-aunt Betty would give me a $50 savings bond. I didn't even know what a savings bond was nor did I understand it then. But guess what—I remember those savings bonds from my childhood more than whatever toys I would have gotten instead.

Continuing with my 50/25/25 rule, 25% of what Caroline's kids earned they can spend on whatever they want. Want that cool new Xbox game or fancy pair of sneakers? Cool—go stuff boxes! This teaches kids to value things more: they make a direct connection between what they want, and how much they have to work to get it. This makes them work harder, and also want to buy less junk that doesn't make them happy anyway. (Hopefully, they'll also want to buy less junk, and invest more, when they see the differential between the long-run value of the junk itself, versus the stock value of the companies that make the junk.)

Finally, the last part in the 50/25/25—they give 25% of what they earn. This teaches them the power of contribution and to be grateful for the blessings they enjoy in life.

Every Christmas season, my mom and I went to Hill's Department Store, which had a Christmas tree with gift requests hanging on it, all written by children from the poorest families in the area.

I asked to pick a name and toy request off the tree. I knew that meant one less toy for me, but it became a meaningful holiday ritual and a reminder that there is someone out there who has it worse than you. Sometimes the family would send a photo back of the little girl or boy with the toy we bought them, and that always meant so much more to me than any toy I unwrapped.

These early lessons taught me the value of generosity. And I believe they were an important part in my own giving and philanthropy once I started to have significant wealth of my own. And why it's a key part of my 50/25/25 rule.

I recommend encouraging your kids to give to causes they can have a direct connection to, such as animals, the environment, children's welfare, or social justice issues they care about. Help get them connected to charities that affect their local community, so they can see the fruits of their giving directly and get involved in other ways. This teaches your children that their hard work can have a tangible impact on the lives of people around them.

One more important benefit of this 50/25/25 approach: When you invest $500 per month per child into the custodial Roth IRAs you set up for them, you can now deduct that from your business. This is yet another tax-advantaged way to support your children and teach them the value of business ownership and investing.

2. Using the "Hummer Loophole" to Write Off Luxury SUVs

After a couple of years in business, I was making more money than I had imagined. I figured it was time to buy my favorite car: a Jeep. This was in 2001, and the car was $28,000. When I was looking at which one to buy, my friend Kelly—who was in college for accounting—told me I can deduct that from my business income, if I was using it for business purposes.

The idea of deducting an SUV sounded crazy to me. But I researched it, and of course she was absolutely correct! I promised myself to never let such a great deduction go to waste again!

In the last decades, I've essentially paid *very little* to own and drive multiple luxury SUVs.

How does it work?

It's something dubbed the "Hummer Loophole." Basically, it means you can take a first-year tax write-off on vehicles that are 6,000 pounds or more in gross weight, proportionate to the amount you use it for business. You can fast-forward your depreciation on the vehicle and deduct up to the entire purchase price in one year, using Sections 179 and 168. The key is, you must use the car for at least 50% of business purposes to take advantage of the deduction; your deduction is proportionate to your business use, up to 100%.

For example, if you buy a $50,000 Chevy Tahoe, and you use it 80% for business, you can write off $40,000 of that vehicle in the first year. Popular SUVs that meet this weight requirement are Chevy Suburbans, Navigators, Escalades, Land Rovers, Porsche Cayennes, and, of course, the loophole's namesake, the Hummer.

Using this method, over the decades I've owned and driven Escalades, Range Rovers, and Infiniti QX80s, costing me essentially nothing on a net basis. How?

First, I let someone else take the depreciation hit of driving the car off the lot. I buy my cars in the sweet spot of a few years old, after the steepest depreciation has passed but before the car gets too old or used. (Current rules allow you to buy a used vehicle for this deduction, so long as it's "new to you," meaning you didn't already own it before.)

Then, I take the first-year tax-write-off of about 80% of the purchase price.

Because I'm in a high tax bracket, the tax write-off I get is worth more to me than the depreciation on the vehicle over the next few years. Once the depreciation on the vehicle starts to get close to the amount I saved in taxes, I sell it. Then rinse, wash, and repeat: I pay essentially nothing for driving some of the nicest SUVs in the world. (If you choose to take advantage of this, make sure you talk to your accountant before you trade or sell it to avoid paying recapture tax.) And remember rules change constantly so although this one has been around for ages, you always want to discuss with a tax strategist.

Here's a cool bonus tip: If your business has a brick-and-mortar location you travel to from your home, you may be able to take advantage of something called a Qualified Accountable Plan. Using this setup, you can legally claim part of your primary residence as a home office, and you can deduct mileage between your home office and your brick-and-mortar location as part of the business use of your car. *Talk to an experienced pro on this one.*

3. The Augusta Rule: Rent Your Personal House to Your Business, Deduct the Rent, and Pay No Rental Income Tax

Every year, tens of thousands of golf fans descend on the small-ish city of Augusta, Georgia, for the Masters golf tournament. All the hotels and motels get booked out way in advance. Because demand for lodging is so high, for decades many locals would rent out their homes during that week for exorbitant fees (sometimes as much as $10,000 a day). This was going on long before Airbnb.

Congress took note of this, and wanted to levy high taxes on all the homeowners earning windfall profits during this one week.

In the 1970s, a bunch of homeowners lobbied Congress. The result was allowing the homeowners to rent their personal residences for up to 14 days tax free. This is enshrined in IRS Section 280A, aka the "Augusta Rule."

Here's the cool part. If you're a homeowner, you don't need to live in Augusta to take advantage of it, nor do you need to rent your home out to strangers during sporting events!

Instead, you can rent your home out to *your own business* for up to 14 days!

Looking for an off-site location for your next corporate business event, retreat, or all-hands meeting? Here's a great place:

Your own home!

You can rent your primary residence to your LLC or S corp for 14 nonconsecutive days in any year, and deduct the rental cost from your business. (You can't do this with a sole proprietorship or a single-member LLC.) You want to have a rental contract and charge prevailing market rates for event space. Call around to local hotels and see what they would charge for an event space that would hold a comparable amount of people.

Let's say you have 10 employees, and once a month you host a daylong strategy and planning session for them. And let's say your local Marriot tells you an event room to host 10 people would cost you $2,000 per day. That means you can pay yourself $2,000 per day (in this case, $28,000 per year), deduct it from the business, and you don't have to pay any personal tax on that.

It's yet one more massive tax advantage for owning your own business.

Are you starting to see a pattern here?

Now before we wrap this tax section up, I want to cover a three more topics.

Income Tax vs. Capital Gains Tax

De Minimis Safe Harbor

Alternate Minimum Tax

Let's look into each a little more.

Income Tax vs. Capital Gains Tax

If you don't fully understand the difference between income tax and capital gains, you are not alone. Every year, millions of people find themselves wondering the same thing.

And no wonder, the difference between capital gains vs. ordinary income tax isn't always obvious, but it can have a *significant* impact on the amount of money you owe in taxes each year.

Let's take a closer look at the difference between these taxes and their potential impact on your finances.

The easiest way to think about capital gains vs. income tax is to see income tax as a federally mandated fee that's levied on any monies that you've earned—through work and personal effort such as wages.

Capital gains taxes are charged on sums that you've earned as a profit through the buying of an asset—such as a vacation home or stocks—and subsequent sale of the asset for a higher price. A realized capital gain is the money from the sale of the asset at a price higher than the one you paid for it. If your asset goes up in price but you do not sell it, you have not "realized" your capital gain and therefore owe no tax.

And to go one step deeper, capital gains taxes fall into two buckets: long term and short term.

Long-term capital gains—which are taxed at a more favorable rate—are charged on assets you have sold after holding them for at least a year. Short-term capital gains are instead charged at the standard higher ordinary income tax rate. Investors have a big incentive to hold appreciated assets for at least a year and a day, qualifying them as long-term assets. Long-term capital gains are given lower preferential tax rates of 10%, 15%, or 20%, depending on your income level.

For 2022, if you are filing single, thresholds are:

10% if your income is less than $41,675;

15% if your income is $459,750 or less;

20% if your income exceeds that amount.

On the other hand, the US income tax system has rates ranging from 10% to 37% of yearly income. Rates also rise as income rises with lower-income individuals being taxed at lower rates than higher-income taxpayers.

Income thresholds for 2022 are:

- 10% on income up to $10,275;
- 12% on income over $10,275;
- 22% on income over $41,775;
- 24% on income over $89,075;
- 32% on income over $170,050;
- 35% on income over $215,950;
- 37% on income over $539,900.

Here's why this is important to know.

The IRS taxes long-term capital gains for high earners—which is how wealthy people make most of their money—at 20%.

Meaning, anyone earning $459,750 in capital gains income is going to pay 20% tax. But if they are making that same amount of $459,750 in earned income, they'll pay 35% tax—that's a difference of $68,962.50 in federal tax alone.

Or another way to look at it is you can make $1,000,000 in the stock market or on real estate and you'd pay 20% tax, which is a lower tax rate than someone who makes $41,775 at their nine-to-five job paying 22%.

No one tells you this when you first start investing, so I personally learned it the hard way. I had bought a house I was intending to hold as a rental—but after my first couple of experiences as a landlord I realized that wasn't for me. I decided to flip the property and put it up for sale. It sold within a month, and of course I was thrilled. However, when I went to file taxes that year and my CPA gave me the amount of taxes I owed. I was shocked. Not only was the sale of the house taxed at the regular income tax rate (and *not* gains rate of 20%) but the sale of the house took me into the highest tax bracket and cost me even more.

This is why investing is so important for you and for your ability to build wealth.

I break down the ways to avoid and reduce capital gains taxes—including how to use the 1031 exchange and the primary residence exclusion—in detail in Chapter 17.

De Minimis Safe Harbor Election and the Dreaded Alternate Minimum Tax

One area of the tax code that brings up a lot of questions is the de minimis safe harbor election. This election is an important one because it permits property owners, landlords, and business owners to deduct the cost of property items used regardless of whether they are a repair or capital improvement, which results in immediate tax savings.

De minimis safe harbor allows most businesses to deduct costs of less expensive items. I don't want to get into the weeds on this one, so I'm just going to cover it at a super high level.

If your business has financial statements (which it should), the de minimis safe harbor election is up to $5,000 per item or invoice. Meaning if you buy a computer for $3,800 and a printer for $1,000, you would be able to take the deduction at a 100% write-off in the year that you purchase it—regardless of whether you put it into service or not.

If you don't have proper financial statements, the de minimis safe harbor election is a $2,500 maximum per item.

It cannot be used for things such as land, inventory, certain types of equipment, and other exclusions.

De minimis safe harbor is a term to know and something to discuss with your tax professional.

And not to further confuse anyone just stepping into this world, because the tax code and tax law is horribly confusing on its own, but to make matters worse, there is something called the alternate minimum tax, or AMT.

You can be aggressive with your tax planning strategy and take all of the deductions I've mentioned in this book. However, the IRS has laid out something specific just for us called the alternate minimum tax.

In summary, the AMT will basically require you to pay a minimum amount of tax regardless of the deductions and credits allowed on your return. The alternative minimum tax (AMT) is a separate tax system that requires some taxpayers to calculate their tax liability twice—first, under ordinary income tax rules, then under the AMT—and pay whichever amount is highest.

In my opinion, it's one of the shittiest parts of the tax code and can be triggered by things such as large capital gains, large itemized deductions, taking a net operating loss in a business, for certain types of installment sales, interest income on certain bonds, or just having high household income.

It's just one more reason why you want to take every single tax deduction, tax break, and loophole possible and always use a tax strategist when doing your tax preparation and planning.

As a business owner, you contribute in many ways. You create products and services that make people's lives better. You create opportunities for your employees and help them support their families. And yes, you pay taxes.

But one way you do *not* need to contribute is paying *more* tax than you have to pay because you weren't aware of how to legally minimize your taxes—until now.

Previous chapters taught *wealth habits* geared toward how to *earn more*. This chapter was all about earning more's often neglected sibling: *keeping* more.

As I hope you see now, earning more isn't as valuable if you're giving away large chunks of it needlessly to the IRS.

Remember, the IRS has one core function: to take as much of your hard-earned money as possible. The government then funnels that money toward a bunch of uses and causes, some of which you support, and some of which you hate.

I'm all for being generous with your money. In fact, it's a cornerstone of my approach to building real wealth and true happiness. (You'll learn more about that in the last chapter.)

But it's a lot easier to give more to people and causes you care about, if you haven't "given" huge chunks of your money away unnecessarily to the IRS, just because you didn't know all the rules. (And part of the reason you didn't know the rules is that the IRS doesn't *want* you to know the rules.)

Why else would the tax code be millions of words that requires hiring a tax professional just to understand it.

Tax strategy is important in building *wealth habits* because wealth isn't just how much money you make, it's also how much money you *keep*.

CHAPTER 14

Trusts Aren't Just for the Rich Kids Anymore

"Trusts are generally thought of only for the rich; however, they are very customizable vehicles that anyone can use depending on their goals."

When you hear the word "trust," you might think of wealthy parents giving their spoiled kids a big chunk of cash and a house in Dorado on their 18th birthday. But trusts aren't just for the rich.

A trust is an estate planning tool that can serve more purposes than most realize. Anyone can use them to ensure their assets are passed down as they wish, to friends, family, or a charity.

I'm going to unpack this and boil it all down in this chapter.

You may have no need for this right now, *but* as you practice the wealth habits in this book and get on the right path to growing your wealth—I want you to bookmark this section on trusts because you may need it later.

Trusts really fall into two categories: irrevocable or revocable.

What's the difference between them?

A **revocable trust** is a living trust where you still have control of your assets.

An **irrevocable trust** is one where you install a trustee who controls the assets, and now you no longer have control.

Generally speaking, if you are not already wealthy, you likely won't want an irrevocable trust.

But even if you're not there right now, I know you're on your way. So let's review them both.

There are three roles (people) involved in trusts:

1. **The grantor:** the person who creates the trust and puts the assets (life insurance policies, properties, bank, and retirement accounts) into the trust.
2. **The trustee:** the person who follows the trust's rules, handles the administration of the trust, and oversees direction/instruction.
3. **The beneficiary:** the person (or organization) who receives the trust's assets and/or income.

Can one person be all of these?

In a revocable trust, yes. But in an irrevocable trust, no.

Ten Benefits of Trusts to Help You and Your Family

Here are some of the benefits a trust can provide:

- Avoid probate;
- Transfer your business without interruption;
- Transfer real estate smoothly to your heirs;
- Provide protection from creditors and lawsuits;
- Leave assets to a child who is still a minor;
- Control inheritance payout amounts;
- Provide for a special-needs child;
- Gift money to charity;
- Provide privacy from public court documents;
- Provide protection in times of illness or disability.

A trust, when established with professional help, may be a useful financial planning tool in each of these situations. Let's look at each more closely.

When we look at trusts in general, both revocable and irrevocable can provide you many of the same things:

1. **Avoids probate (which can be lengthy and costly):**

    When you use a will to transfer your estate's assets, a court is involved in settling and distributing them. This process is called probate—the process of settling one's estate.

It can take six, eight, or even twelve months or more to complete the process. It might also involve extensive paperwork, court hearings, and attorney's fees, aka lots of money and time.

Also, because court documents become public record, probate makes a family's private financial matters public. Placing assets in a trust while you are still alive can not only reduce attorney and administration expenses, but it can maintain your privacy.

2. Transfers your business without interruption:

Placing your business into a trust will allow it to continue to operate. Without it, your business can also get tied up in probate, interrupting or even halting business activities. Making sure you have enough insurance coverage to repay personal debt and/or any estate taxes when you die may help prevent creditors from pursuing your business assets. The last thing any business owner wants is to have their heirs have to sell the business just to pay for final expenses.

If you currently have a business, what is your succession plan?

3. Transfers real estate smoothly to your heirs:

Transferring real estate to a trust can not only keep it out of probate but may be able to help prevent it from being reassessed for property tax purposes because you do not have a change in ownership in the underlying real estate.

On the other hand, transferring real property into an irrevocable trust can actually trigger a reassessment because this is a change in ownership and may result in higher property taxes. Additional considerations apply for mortgaged properties. Because laws greatly vary by state, it's important to get professional advice before transferring real estate to a trust.

The process itself is straightforward. A quitclaim or grant deed can be used to transfer real estate ownership from an individual to a trust. A notary witnesses the documents' signing, and the local government records the change in ownership after receiving the paperwork. Real estate insurance policies should be updated to name the trust as beneficiary. Talk to your financial professional in advance to make sure this won't be a problem and that you have appropriate coverage. Keep in mind that there may also be gift tax implications when you transfer real estate to a trust and a lot of this varies from state to state. Always consult an estate or trust attorney in your area to find out more.

4. Provides protection from creditors and lawsuits (for your assets):

While a revocable living trust, the kind you might use to avoid probate, will typically not protect assets from creditors and lawsuits, a properly structured irrevocable trust can. When you use this type of trust, however, you must permanently give up your ownership interest in the assets you place into it and your control over those assets.

Taking it a step further, an irrevocable life insurance trust may be a valuable planning tool for high-net-worth individuals and couples seeking to mitigate estate taxes and maximize wealth transfer to their heirs. Most people consult a financial professional when considering such an option.

5. **Leaves assets to a minor child:**

One option for giving assets to a minor is a 2503(c) trust, named after the relevant section of the tax code. This trust allows an adult to control the use of the trust property until the beneficiary turns 21. It can reduce the grantor's estate taxes and shift taxable income to a minor child who has a lower tax rate than the grantor. A downside is that the grantor loses control of the assets when the beneficiary turns 21.

A trust set up for a child's benefit can be either a simple trust or a complex trust. These are legal terms that determine whether the trust must distribute all its income each year (simple) or not (complex).

A complex trust can provide greater protection should the child have behavioral or substance abuse problems. It's always advisable to seek out a lawyer to set up such a trust.

6. **Controls inheritance payout amounts:**

With a spendthrift trust, you can make sure your beneficiaries do not squander their inheritance or have it attached by creditors. A trustee controls the trust's assets and parcels them out to the beneficiary over time in accordance with the trust's terms.

This type of trust can, for example, be used to help provide for and protect an adult child who is not good with money, who suffers from an addiction to drugs or gambling, or who later gets a divorce. The grantor can require the trustee to give the beneficiary a certain amount of money from the trust each month, or give the trustee the discretion to withhold benefits under certain circumstances, among other possibilities.

7. **Provides for a special-needs child:**

Children and adults with special needs may be eligible for Supplemental Security Income and Medicaid, two federal benefits that help with living and medical expenses for individuals who can't support themselves fully or at all.

Leaving assets directly to a special-needs child can jeopardize eligibility for these benefits. Instead, creating a special-needs trust controlled by someone who is not the beneficiary can maintain benefit eligibility and provide for your child in your absence.

8. **Gifts money to charity:**

There are two types of trusts that can be used to facilitate gifts to charity: charitable remainder trusts and charitable lead trusts. Both are irrevocable trusts, which require you to give up control of the assets placed in the trust, and both can provide income tax deductions and estate tax mitigation.

The remainder trust provides current income payments to the grantor followed by payment of the remaining trust balance to a charity, while the lead trust provides current income payments to a charity followed by payment of the remainder interest to a non-charitable beneficiary.

Complexities surrounding which types of assets to place in a charitable trust, the tax deductions tied to each, and other matters make professional help invaluable.

9. **Provides privacy from public court documents:**

A trust is able to protect you and your family's privacy by keeping assets out of probate. Once your legal documents go to probate, they are public records, and public records can be viewed by anyone. It adds that extra layer of protection. If the trust owns your home or other assets that are in county records, and someone tried to search to find out more information on you, where you live or what assets you own—those searches will be less likely to find your name and private information on the first page of Google.

10. **Provides protection in times of illness or disability:**

Wills only go into effect upon someone's death, but a trust established during your lifetime can also help your family if you become ill or unable to manage your assets. Though no one likes to think about these scenarios, building in provisions like these can safeguard your family from having to make decisions without knowing your wishes during difficult times.

How an Irrevocable Trust Is Different

There are three main reasons you'd want to give up control of your assets and create an irrevocable trust:

1. Minimize estate taxes (your heirs—kids, family, charity—pay less when you die);
2. Eligibility for government programs (Medicare);
3. Protection from creditors.

If you don't have significant wealth *yet*, there is likely no good reason to have an irrevocable trust. In 2022, there is no federal estate tax below $12.06 million per spouse or $24.12 million per couple, which means the main reason to have an irrevocable trust would be to shield assets—over this amount—from the grubby hands of the IRS. (State estate taxes can be much lower, so you always want to check your state as well.)

And just remember, should you decide an irrevocable trust is for you, be cautious with whom you make your trustee and your beneficiary as the document cannot be changed. If your middle child is named a beneficiary and they start making some poor decisions in their life, you can't decide to remove them. An irrevocable trust cannot be terminated or changed, unless the beneficiaries agree.

If you want something that can help you avoid probate, save costs on estate administration (attorney fees), and protect your privacy—you'd likely be well served with a revocable trust for all of that. Whether you use a revocable or irrevocable, consider a Trust Protector. A trust protector might be a third party who makes a decision or a change to a trust when the primary purpose or an interpretation is needed.

I'm typically all for a DIY approach, but when it comes to legal issues—especially navigating the complexities of a trust—meet with an experienced attorney in estate planning. Choosing an estate planning attorney who has sufficient knowledge and experience and works to determine your needs, goals, and family situation will be invaluable in setting this up correctly. Make sure to tell your attorney about any digital assets you own as well. This could be NFTs, websites, podcasts, courses, or other digital assets. You'll want to add provisions within the will or trust to cover these types of assets as well.

For many families, owning a home and having retirement savings are keys to building generational wealth. Ensuring those assets are protected and can be passed to your heirs without losing a significant amount of it is essential to caring for your family.

Wealth isn't about buying fancy cars and vacation homes and taking amazing trips. Although it may afford you to do those things, far more importantly, if it's done correctly, it will allow you to care for the people you love, even after you're gone.

CHAPTER 15

The Brinks Truck of Your Finances— Security and Protection

You know the Brinks armored cars that deliver cash to all the banks and big box stores? Think of *security* as the Brinks truck for your financial life.

Security protects you and your family against the unexpected, and unwanted, life events—the death of a loved one, a medical emergency, or losing a job—and unexpected financial hardship.

The security vehicle provides you with a financial airbag that softens the blow of a crisis. This protects you if, or most likely when, an unexpected or unwanted financial challenge comes up and can buy you some time to get back on your feet and give you peace of mind amidst challenge.

This may not be the sexiest chapter in the book, but it's an important one—and one that you can take action on right away.

Four Ways to Get the Security and Protection You Need

You never know when you will be sitting enjoying a cup of coffee, on a sunset stroll with your dog, or having a seemingly normal, usual day at work and you get the call no one wants—or expects—to ever get.

Your dad was in a motorcycle accident, your business caught on fire, you were just told you lost your job, or got the devastating news that a loved one passed away.

Wealth habits isn't just about spending less and earning more—it's also about saving more. Let's dive into the four ways you save *yourself* from financial disaster and create that Brinks truck for your life.

1. Protect Your Life with 6–12 Months' Worth of Income Saved

Having an emergency fund is personal finance 101. Regardless of who you talk to in the finance and investing world, this is a cardinal rule. Unless you already have a high net worth and numerous assets (that can be liquidated easily), this is a critical step for financial security and stability.

If you look through decades and decades of financial data, you'll see no market has ever shot straight up forever. There are always dips and pullbacks, always challenges and seasons of winter. There will always be the unexpected. The only way you can try to avoid it is to plan for it so you can get out of any negative situation with the least amount of damage.

That's why it is crucial to have 6–12 months of cash on hand.

This is the only money you really want to have liquid. This money is set aside and saved inside of a high-yield savings account or a money market type of brokerage account (not your main checking account or business account).

Here's the formula for the minimum six months:

If you are making roughly $5,000 a month, and you want to start with the minimum of six months emergency funds, you would need to have at least $30,000 saved (6 × $5,000).

If you are single and on your own, or single with dependents, you may want to make sure you have at least 12 months of income to fall back on. The goal of this fund—should you face job loss, physical injury, be in an accident and temporarily unable to work—is to carry you through. This needs to be highly liquid and easy to access should you need it. Do not touch it for other investments or purchases.

One way to factor how many months you need is to look at how many months, approximately, it would take to replace your job if you lost it or couldn't work.

If you think you could find a job quickly, then perhaps six months is plenty for you. But if you are not in a high-demand market or in a business that is cyclical or can easily change with market trends, then you may want to consider more than 12 months saved just in case of emergency.

Just remember that this money should not be tied into your primary checking account, which pays you no interest at all. You want this to be in a separate account that's interest bearing. Most brokerage and mutual fund firms will have money market accounts that pay a little bit more interest than your typical savings or interest-bearing checking account—it won't be much based on current interest rates—but something is better than nothing. To find out rates you can check sites such as **www.bankrate.com** and **www.nerdwallet.com**.

2. Protect Your Business with Key Policies

Insurance isn't a fun or exciting topic, I get it.

But if you've stuck with me this long in the chapter I want to commend you for your dedication to build *wealth habits*. I can already tell you're going to be massively successful in this journey to creating financial freedom.

I gotta tell ya, I am taking a couple of deep breaths as I write this. This specific topic hits close to home. Really close.

It was October 2018. Just a month earlier, I had secured a buyer for one of my businesses, and everything was on track for me to exit by the end of the year.

As a female in business, knowing that only 2% of female-owned businesses break the million-dollar mark, and that less than 0.5% of women in business ever *sell* their companies—those accomplishments meant a lot to me.

At 4 a.m. that fall October morning, I heard yelling, and someone was beating on the door to my house. It took a minute to come out of a dead sleep to try and figure out what was happening.

"A fire! It's on fire!" I opened the door and once my eyes came into focus, I saw my mom and asked, "Mom, what?" trying to figure out what was going on, "What fire?" She replied, "The spa! It's all on fire!"

I grabbed my shoes and jumped in the car. As we crested the top of the hill, I could see the plume of smoke above the town—instantly I knew. It's gone.

In one moment, everything flashed in front of my eyes—a multi-million dollar business I worked so hard to build, the first commercial building I was able to build with my dad; dozens of my employees who were coming to work that day; thousands of our loyal clients; the buyer who was about to buy the business; another buyer purchasing the commercial building I owned next door—over 20 years of hard work and memories, up in flames.

No one thinks it can happen to them, until it *does*.

And yes, I rebuilt. I made sure my employees weren't out of work, our clients were taken care of, and yes, I secured another buyer—but it wasn't easy.

In fact, it was absolute hell. And I don't want you to ever have to go through what I did. And *especially* not underinsured.

I'll spare you the endless blood, sweat, and tears of that period of time—but it's important I say this: Please take this seriously. It may not be a fun, flashy read, but I promise it's important to hear, and at least consider, what you need to create your own Brinks truck and what protection and security you need to beef up in your own life.

Business Owner's Policy

A business owner's policy is an affordable way to buy small business insurance.

It usually bundles general liability insurance, commercial property insurance, and business interruption insurance together (Lazarony, 2021).

Business liability insurance can pay for your legal costs, along with settlements and judgments. It may also help your small business to maintain financial stability, if you get sued. If you're responsible for someone's injuries (not employee's injuries), insurance pays for medical bills and lost wages, too. It also covers other claims like reputational harm, advertising injury, and copyright infringement.

Business interruption insurance is important to have as it replaces lost income if you need to temporarily shut down due to a loss covered by the policy like theft, lightning strike, or damaged merchandise.

Commercial property insurance covers both owned and leased business equipment as well as office records, outdoor fixtures such as signs, and losses due to vandalism, among others.

You may think you'll never use it, but trust me when I tell you—no one does. I didn't either. But please be smarter than I was. Have a yearly meeting with your insurance agent to make sure the coverage limits in place are high enough for where you currently are in your business. It's one of the things I failed to do. I was underinsured and it ended up costing me hundreds of thousands if not millions of dollars.

Key Person's Policy

Key person insurance is a life insurance policy a company purchases on the life of an owner, top executive, or key employee considered critical to the business.

The company is the beneficiary of the policy and pays the premiums. Key person insurance offers a financial cushion if the sudden loss of a certain individual would have a profound negative effect on the company's operations.

This type of policy is often overlooked although could be critical to your business. A key person's policy provides a death benefit that essentially buys the company time to find a new person, offsets lost income from the cancellation of a business project involving a key person, and allows surviving shareholders to purchase the business assets of the deceased. Key person insurance can give the company some options during otherwise difficult times.

Personal Liability Umbrella (PLU)

If you have assets, or any kind of wealth, this is one policy you don't want to ignore.

If you were ever to be sued for more than your existing home, auto, or business insurance will pay—you could lose all your assets. Umbrella insurance is designed to protect you.

Let's say your dog bolts out of the house, bites a neighbor and you get sued for medical bills. Or you send sandwiches to your son's school for a field trip lunch and everyone gets food poisoning and sues. Or your teenager throws a party at your house and someone brings alcohol. One of the kids is arrested for driving under the influence—and you're sued (Fontinelle, 2021).

Umbrella insurance even covers certain liability claims your other policies may not, like slander, false imprisonment, malicious prosecution, wrongful entry, invasion of privacy, and other hazards. PLUs aren't that expensive and can protect you when your other policies can't.

Directors and Officers (D&O) Insurance

This type of liability insurance policy covers the decisions made by directors and officers and board members on the company's behalf. If they're sued, D&O insurance can pay defense costs or a settlement. Accusations can include mismanagement of funds, discrimination suits, slander, and theft of intellectual property, to name a few (Metz, 2022). If you sit on any boards, or are an officer for a nonprofit, make sure they have a D&O policy in place so you aren't taking on any unnecessary liability.

There are other policies that business owners may want to get familiar with—Worker's Comp, Cyber Liability, Product Liability, Errors & Omissions—your need, if any, will depend on the variables and risk in your business. You can find more on my website **www.candyvalentino.com**.

3. Protect Your Family with Life Insurance

Although the subject of life insurance may be the dullest ever, it's still important—especially if someone depends on you and/or your income. If you are married, if you have kids, if you are a single parent, if you are responsible for a special-needs child or sibling, this is a step you can't skip over.

Nobody wants to be over-insured and pay more than they need to, but life insurance is also not a place to cut corners—especially if you have dependents.

The question is, how much do you actually need?

Take a look at all of the major loans and financial debts you have:

What would it cost to pay off your house? _____

Your cars/personal loans? _____

Do you have a second mortgage? _____

Mortgages on any other vacation/second homes? _____

Do you have business debt? Commercial loans? _____

You also want to think about funeral expenses, estate taxes, and any types of probate costs (these can add up and be tens of thousands of dollars if you don't have the right estate plan in place). _____

Total: _____

This is really only a starting point, because depending on the number of dependents you have, your family living situation, and the ages of your kids, you may need a significant amount of insurance for their protection.

Suppose that you have no dependents; in that case, you might limit your life insurance to simply covering expenses like funeral costs, estate taxes, and probate. Or you can get a larger policy and bequest the death benefit to charities that are important to you, like I am doing.

Life insurance in general is extremely confusing because there are so many different types of policies—like hundreds. Because of the complexities, insurance as a whole is widely misunderstood. And the people who know the most are also the ones selling it to you!

I want to keep the insurance topic super simple and classify it into two different types, **term and permanent**.

Term Insurance

The insurance known as term life insurance is a popular choice with characteristics that are easy to understand.

It's called term because the policy has a term—usually 10, 20, or 30 years—and a monthly premium. Term insurance provides a death benefit but does not have any "cash benefit."

As long as you keep paying the premium during the term of the policy, and if you happen to die during that time, the beneficiary will receive the predetermined amount upon your death.

These premiums are way less than any other policy. However, you may outlive the term and will need a new one. The premium cost of a term policy is factored at the age you are when applying for a new plan. The older you are, the higher the premium.

Term insurance is not an investment. You get inexpensive coverage and pay premiums every month for a specific number of years. If you haven't died before the term is up, you get nothing. If you do die, your dependents receive the death benefit payout.

I'll simplify it even further: If you haven't yet built wealth, term insurance is the way to go.

Once you have built wealth, there are certain types of insurance policies that can have tax benefits and can create leverage when building assets—which brings us to permanent life insurance.

Permanent Life

Permanent life policies are more complicated than term policies but can potentially offer tax and investment benefits.

With a cash-value life insurance policy, a portion of each premium you pay goes toward insuring your life, another portion goes to the insurance company, and the rest goes toward building up a cash value.

Depending on the type of policy, it can gain interest or be invested, and that income grows without the IRS getting their dirty paws on it.

If you later want to withdraw any portion of this cash value, you pay tax on the gains then. But you've had the benefit of years or decades of tax-deferred compounding growth before that time.

In addition, you can take out a loan from this cash value, and—like all loans—you don't pay tax on it. You can pay the loan back while you're alive, or it can be subtracted from the death benefit.

Cash-value life insurance is not limited to one type of life insurance and it can get *really* complicated. That's in part because it can serve two distinct purposes. Not only does this insurance provide the usual benefit of payment to your beneficiaries if and when you die, but it also acts as an investment account of sorts.

I don't want to get too deep into this because it's quite tedious (not to mention boring!). But I do want to give you general information, for building your knowledge and understanding.

Again, I'm going to make a broad sweeping statement—if you haven't built wealth yet, stick with term insurance. Focus on building your knowledge about investing—build wealth through investing in the markets, not through buying insurance policies.

In the permanent life category, there are numerous types, but let's cover a couple of the most common.

Whole Life

In short, you pay a monthly premium like a term policy— only these rates are much, much more because a portion of that monthly fee is "invested," so it can accumulate and earn dividends. As a result, the value of your policy builds, and you can borrow against the value or cash out by canceling the coverage.

The reason you'll hear these are a bad investment is because the return on your money is so low it may not even keep up with inflation.

Now let's assume you're 40 years old and looking for coverage. Your hypothetical choices are a 30-year term life policy with an annual premium of $500 versus a whole life policy with an annual premium of $3,000—for the same death benefit. If you take the term life policy—saving yourself $2,500 a year in premiums—and invest that steadily in stocks with an average annual return of 7% (that's actually a few percentage points below the average), keep investing that amount, and you'll have almost $250,000 in 30 years.

Even if you were to invest your $2,500 annual savings more conservatively, at a 3% average annual return, you'd be sitting on about $119,000. And as long as you'd invested that money in an IRA or 401(k), you'd get the same tax-deferred growth that a whole life policy promises. And in some cases like a Roth IRA, that growth will actually be tax free.

Generally speaking, if you have the ability to pay the whole life premiums, you have the means to put those same funds into retirement plans or other investments and get better returns.

Universal Life

Universal life is similar to whole life in the fact it provides a death benefit and has a cash value. In short, universal life is trying to act like term insurance and an investment account.

The monthly premium is basically split. Part of the premium supports the death benefit while the other part becomes your "savings" investment. With a universal life policy, you may hope that the investment grows over time, but in reality, the fees are pretty hefty and the return on your investment is not. You may be better off following my suggestion above by getting a term policy and investing the rest.

Variable Universal Life

Whole life and universal life policies may have two distinct purposes, but variable universal life policies have three! They act as regular life insurance (with a death benefit) and a savings account, but also add the aspects of a mutual fund. #overachiever

Variable life insurance has separate accounts containing investment funds such as stocks, bonds, equity funds, money market funds, and bond funds. These policies have specific tax benefits, like the tax-deferred accumulation of earnings and policyholders may access the cash value via a tax-free loan—and unpaid loans, including principal and interest, reduce the death benefit.

With a variable universal life policy, you can decide *how* the policy invests your cash value. That's the "variable" part. The investment subaccounts allow you to invest the cash value and functions similar to a mutual fund. Because it's invested in the market, it has more risk but also has more potential upside if it performs well.

Keep in mind that *you* may control how and where the policy invests your money, but the catch is that *you*—instead of the insurance company—carry the risk of your chosen investments.

Indexed Universal Life (IUL)   Just like whole life and universal life, which are doing two things at once, indexed universal life is as well—only this cash value portion is invested in an index fund.

It ties your cash value to the performance of an index, such as the S&P 500.

This type of policy tends to have lower premiums than other forms of whole life insurance *but* comes with some hefty fees. These fees can drain your policy's cash value during market downturns.

IULs are exempt from federal regulation so they are not regulated by the US Securities and Exchange Commission, unlike stocks and options.

Even once you have built wealth, it's important to do your research. IULs are definitely more advanced and more complicated. You'll want to evaluate death benefit, underlying index, cap rate, participation rate, spread rate, bonuses, cost of insurance, charges, and cash flow capabilities in the form of policy withdrawals and tax-free loans.

4. Protect Your Income with Disability Insurance

Coming in last—disability insurance.

I have to admit, I used to think disability insurance was a waste.

Most Americans have life insurance, but a much smaller percentage have disability insurance. It wasn't that long ago that I changed my opinion on this.

I was in Cabo writing this very book you are holding in your hands when I got the call no one ever wants to get. "Your dad was in a motorcycle accident." A driver in another vehicle blew through a stop sign.

Her car hit my dad's motorcycle, ejecting him and his girlfriend into the air, landing on the pavement below. They were both life-flighted to a trauma hospital located in the city about 30 miles away.

He suffered injuries to the right side of his body—seven broken ribs, five broken bones in his shoulder, a broken clavicle, broken fingers, collapsed lung, internal bleeding, and bruises all over his body. It was an absolute miracle he survived.

His girlfriend suffered a broken rib, a broken ankle that required surgery, and injuries to her shoulder, to name a few.

My dad has been riding motorcycles for 25+ years and rarely wore a helmet, but his decision to wear one that day saved his life.

Even as I write this, the emotions of that day are still really fresh. But I tell you this story because it changed my view on this subject.

After I hung up from that call, I immediately jumped on a plane and flew to the hospital. I was with my dad in the TICU for the next 10 days.

Although my dad had motorcycle insurance and health insurance, he did not have disability insurance. The injuries he sustained were extensive, as were the medical bills. And although the other driver had insurance, it wasn't nearly enough.

He had a chest tube in for 10 days in an effort to control the internal bleeding and fluid around his heart and lung. Even after being discharged, he needed care for months and then more months of therapy, doctor visits, scans, and imaging in hopes to gain use of his shoulder again. The extent of his injuries, and the pain, kept him out of work for months—with no disability insurance to offset any expenses.

On the opposite side of the spectrum, his girlfriend had long-term and short-term disability insurance through her employer. With her short-term coverage, she was able to collect her full income and wages for three months as she recovered. Then, if she needed more time, she had a long-term disability policy that would kick in.

Those policies made a difference of tens of thousands of dollars.

We never think that something life changing is going to happen to us.

In 2020, the National Center for Vital Statistics reported **3.4 million** deaths; however, according to the Insurance Information Institute, approximately 54% of Americans are covered by some type of life insurance which is equivalent to **179.2 million.**

On the contrary, the CDC reports **39.5 million** medically consulted injuries in the US annually and **241 million** car accidents per year. But according to the Council for Disability Awareness there are only **89.9 million** Americans who have disability insurance—less than half of those who have life insurance—even though your chance of serious injury is more than 10 times greater than dying!

Had my dad had disability insurance, his living expenses would've been taken care of while he recovered for months on end.

It's a lesson for all of us that without disability insurance, we face the risk that a serious injury or illness will wipe out a big chunk of the wealth we're trying to create, which is also why having an emergency fund is so critical.

Disability insurance is not a vehicle to create wealth. Instead, it is simply a protection plan for your current earnings. This is one of those things we tend to put off, including me, until something like this happens. Don't wait until something goes wrong. By then, it is too late.

With so many different policy options, it can be hard to tell what is necessary and what isn't. Premiums will be based on a number of factors such as age, health, and occupation. Individually purchased policies are more expensive—but you get what you pay for. Whatever policy you get, consider one that has a guaranteed renewal and is non-cancelable. There are of course other things to look for but these two are significant.

Protecting yourself and your family shouldn't be left to chance, and it's something you can't ignore. It's an intentional and important step not just in building your wealth, but in building and protecting your life.

CHAPTER 16

Give Yourself the Opportunity to Retire Early—and Rich

D o you remember the reason most businesses fail? Lack of planning.

Do you know the reason most people fail to retire at the wealth level they want—or even retire at all? Lack of planning.

Very few people get in cars and just start driving with no idea where they're going or how they're going to get there.

Yet most people think they're going to retire successfully—*without having a plan for how they're going to get there!*

Just like you need a plan if you're going to start a business, and just like you need a map if you're going to drive on a long trip to a place you've never been, this chapter will help you create the plan and map to your own retirement.

Most people assume planning for retirement is complicated and difficult, and perhaps that's because some financial planners and other professionals in the field talk over our heads in complex terms, which makes you rely on them—and of course they're compensated for your reliance.

But the fact is, if you keep it simple and learn just a few fundamentals, this book pays for itself 100 times over.

Retirement Plans for Business Owners

If you haven't already figured it out, I want you to become as wealthy as you desire and I want the IRS to get as little of your money as possible.

One of the great advantages of being a business owner is that you can use business retirement plans to keep more money away from the IRS than a regular employee can.

I want to cover five of the most common retirement plans and how they relate to you. They are Individual 401(k) (aka solo or self-employed 401(k)), Simplified Employee Pension (SEP), SIMPLE IRA, SIMPLE 401(k), and Roth IRA.

Individual 401(k), Self-Employed (or Solo) 401(k)

The best retirement plan for a business owner who wants to optimize contributions is a 401(k)—individual, or self-employed (solo).

The plan offers **tax-deferred growth**, which means you can reduce your taxable income now—when you contribute to the fund—and you pay taxes later when you withdraw.

When you're self-employed or own a business that employs no others (with the exception of your spouse)—and want to maximize contributions to retirement—this one's for you.

This plan recognizes business owners who participate as both employer and employee. Whether you have a sole proprietorship, partnership, or C or S corporation, you get the largest possible contribution for your retirement plan. (Baldridge, 2022).

Wearing your "employee" hat, you can contribute up to 100% of your salary (if you receive a W-2 from your corporation), or up to 100% of your net adjusted business income, to a maximum of $20,500 or $27,000 if you're at least age 50.

Next, we move you from "employee" to "business owner." Sole proprietors or single member LLCs, enjoy an employer profit sharing contribution of (at most) 20%. The highest employer profit sharing contribution for C or S corporations earning a W-2 is 25%.

The irafinancialgroup.com site indicates that, in 2022, the solo 401(k) plan contributions (including those for employee deferrals and employer profit sharing), top out at $61,000 for those below 50 years of age, and $67,500 for those aged 50 or older.

A key difference with the solo 401(k) is that you can make higher contributions at lower income levels—thanks to the "employee" contribution. And a perk with a solo 401(k), your "employee" contribution can be taxed like a Roth IRA, meaning you pay tax on it now, but it's tax-free upon distribution.

With a solo 401(k), unlike with a SEP, you can take out a loan equal to the lesser of 50% of the plan balance, or $50,000.

Depending on your business structure, your contributions will either be considered a business expense (if you're incorporated) or will be a deduction from your personal income (if you're unincorporated).

A solo 401(k) is currently the best retirement plan you can set up when you're self-employed. A key benefit of the solo 401(k) plan is the high contribution limit, which did go up significantly in 2022. Also, when you consider the Roth option, the loan feature, and the alternative investment potential, the individual 401(k) or solo 401(k) is a great plan for anyone eligible.

Seriously consider talking with a financial planner or other professional to help you establish a 401(k) plan if you have any type of self-employment income.

SEP IRA

A Simplified Employee Pension (SEP) IRA is different than a self-employed 401(k) in how it can cover employees and give you more flexibility as your business grows. This type of plan is available for a variety of small-business structures, including sole proprietorships, partnerships, LLCs, S corporations, and C corporations and can be an attractive option for a small business with few employees.

You can easily establish and maintain a SEP IRA, and there are typically no costs to set-up or any annual, ongoing fees. SEP IRA plans are funded entirely by the employer; no contributions come from the employees.

You can contribute up to 25% of your earnings to an SEP retirement account. The maximum amount that you can contribute is $61,000 per participant in 2022.

Just note, a drawback is that SEP plans may grow to be expensive if your goal is aggressive saving.

Unlike some other retirement plans, an SEP IRA is created primarily as a vehicle for employer contributions and not payroll deductions. And unlike 401(k) plans, the funds in an SEP IRA cannot be used as collateral for loans.

Like other individual retirement accounts, these contributions are tax deductible. But contribution rates are required to be uniform for all employees of a company that has an SEP IRA plan, including the owner. This means the contribution percentage that you (as the owner) use must be the same contribution percentage that's available for employees.

These plans offer small business owners an opportunity to save much more for their own retirement than they could with a traditional IRA, but again you have to contribute funds for all eligible employees.

SIMPLE IRA

The Savings Incentive Match Plan (SIMPLE) IRA is a great option if you own a business that has fewer than 100 employees and your goal is to set up an IRA for each employee.

With a SIMPLE IRA, the annual contribution for 2022 is limited to $14,000, and age 50 or older can contribute additional funds, up to $17,000 to potentially make up for prior years' lower contributions.

Employers generally match the contributions dollar-for-dollar (up to 3% of the employee's compensation), or they can choose to contribute 2% whether or not the employee decides to add their own money and contribute into the plan.

Employees make contributions to a SIMPLE IRA with pretax wages, which lowers their current taxable income. The invested money grows without being taxed until that money is withdrawn in retirement. At that time, those withdrawals are subject to be taxed as ordinary income.

In addition, contribution limits are higher than the limits granted to traditional or Roth IRAs.

Simple IRA participants are allowed to double their investing efforts with an individual IRA, enabling maximum contributions. And if you plan to tuck away more money for your retirement, you can open another account such as a traditional or Roth IRA.

While the self-employed 401(k), SEP IRA, and SIMPLE IRA represent three plans that are quite effective for small businesses, you have two others to examine, too.

SIMPLE 401(k)

Savings Incentive Match Plan for Employees can come in the form of a SIMPLE IRA or a SIMPLE 401(k).

If you're a small business owner with fewer than 100 employees, you may want to consider a SIMPLE 401(k) plan for your company.

The biggest catch is this: You, the employer, *must make* either:

1. A matching contribution up to 3% of each employee's pay, or
2. A non-elective contribution of 2% of each eligible employee's pay.

Employees can contribute up to $14,000 in 2022. Age 50 and over, you're allowed an additional "catch-up" contribution amount of $3,000 a year.

Employees are totally vested in any and all contributions making a staged vesting plan for employee retention completely useless.

SIMPLE 401(k) plans may also allow loans.

With a regular 401(k) plan, a company must perform costly nondiscrimination testing. This is not true with a SIMPLE 401(k), which makes the administrative burden considerably less.

Make sure you discuss your options and what plan is best for your business based on your business variables—employees, contribution amounts, and objective of the plan—with your financial and tax pro.

Roth IRA

A Roth IRA is available to everyone who has earned income—not just business owners—provided your income falls under the ceiling of eligibility. If you are just starting out on your investment journey and you're eligible for a Roth IRA— this is a really great place to start. The Roth IRA can be one of the very best long-term investment accounts you can have.

Keep this fact in mind about Roth IRA contributions: Although they come from **after-tax income**, these funds **grow tax free** within the account and their **distributions are tax free**, too.

But you'll also find a downside to the Roth IRA. Access to this plan is restricted on the basis of the contributor's income, so high wage earners are excluded.

To be eligible to contribute to a Roth IRA, by 2022 rules, you must have a modified adjusted gross income that's less than $129,000 (if you're single) or $204,000 (if you're married and filing jointly). In addition, once your income climbs to $144,000 (if single) or $214,000 (if married and filing jointly), you are restricted from contributing any money to a Roth IRA (Stewart, 2022).

The maximum contribution to a Roth IRA account for 2022 is $6,000. And when you're 50 and older, you can add an extra $1,000 per year in "catch-up" contributions, bringing the total contribution to $7,000 (Stewart, 2022).

You can withdraw contributions from a Roth anytime, but if you want to withdraw earnings tax free, you must be at least 59½ and have owned the Roth for at least five years.

Roth IRAs can be opened through a bank, brokerage, mutual fund, or insurance company. You can invest your money in stocks, bonds, mutual funds, exchange-traded funds, and other approved investments (but I don't recommend holding it at a bank or credit-union as your returns will be much lower and it won't grow as intended.)

The bottom line is that owning and operating a small business, or a family, or both can feel like an all-consuming endeavor—and I get it—at times it certainly is.

We often put things off in hopes to get to them later, but when you fail to make time to get it done now, you will likely never do it.

Contributing to retirement isn't an option, it's a must. And if you currently don't have enough to start now, you aren't applying the *wealth habits*— you are overspending. Take the time, and have the discipline, to invest in yourself and your future.

Investing in your retirement is a *wealth habit* you have to start now to finish wealthy. Give yourself the opportunity to retire early—and *rich*.

WEALTH HABIT 5

Investing Your Way to Wealth

CHAPTER 17

Real Estate Investing: The Hat Trick of Building Wealth

I don't know much about sports, but I do know about a thing called the "hat trick."

In hockey, a hat trick is when a player scores three goals in one game. But in real estate, a hat trick is your ability to get three distinct benefits from the same investment.

Your money is used to purchase a real asset, and while the asset grows in value, the property **appreciates**. That's goal #1.

While you are renting out that property, you have a business, and now you're able to take advantage of **tax savings**. That's goal #2.

Plus, you can now use it as collateral to buy other assets, get some of your money back if you make improvements or get tenants increasing its value, which enables you to continue building more wealth, which leads us to another great thing: leverage.

Leverage is a simple real estate investing strategy in which investors borrow money to buy property, with the goal of increasing returns and leverage debt for bigger returns. Leveraging increases your return when the interest you pay is less than the return on investment (ROI).

But we still haven't covered the most important part, two magic words: **cash flow**. That's goal #3.

In addition to the hat trick, real estate also has diverse flexibility and some great tax benefits (which we will unpack in a bit).

But first, even beyond all of these reasons—as if those aren't enough— why I like investing in real estate, more than any other kind of investing, are these four words: get more for less.

Only in real estate can I take $1 million of my own money and buy $4 million, $5 million, or even $10 million in assets.

To invest in stocks, my million dollars is only going to buy a million dollars of Tesla, Apple, or some index fund.

But even in a very traditional deal of needing 25% down to buy an investment property—I only need $250,000 of my own money to buy $1 million in assets.

Touchdown. Okay, now I'm mixing my sports, but you get the point.

Over 20 years ago, when I bought my first property, I didn't have hundreds of thousands of dollars, or even tens of thousands of dollars! But I was able to buy a property with the little money I did have and turn it into far more than I could have imagined.

Now, before we get sidetracked, let's break it down in simple form.

I shared with you the REI hat trick but there's a little more to it. Here are the "*Five Ways to Wealth*" and how to build wealth through real estate investing (REI). That's the gist of this chapter. Let's dive deep into each.

REI Way to Wealth #1: Property Appreciation

Property appreciation is the increase of real estate value over time. This occurs because of an increase in demand for that property. As property becomes more scarce, but is still desired, the price for it goes up.

Unlike depreciating assets such as cars, boats, computers, cell phones, and furniture—real estate properties have a strong trend of appreciation, meaning that over time the value of the property increases. Why?

Part of it is inflation, but the other factor is demand. A simple supply and demand principle applies heavily in real estate. We can't magically make any more land on the earth, so as empty land gets used and developed, the occupied land becomes more desirable. When available houses, or land to build housing, is low in any area of the country—it creates a strong demand, creating the value to go up.

According to the US Bureau of Labor Statistics, prices for housing are 857.74% higher in 2022 versus 1967. Home values declined during the recession of 2008 but have since rebounded and hit another all-time high in 2021. In other words, housing that cost $100,000 in 1967 would cost almost $1 million in 2022—$957,742 to be exact.

Between 1967 and 2022: Housing experienced an average inflation rate of 4.19% per year. This rate of change indicates significant inflation.

However, a major fact of real estate is that real estate values are all local to that specific area. Cities such as Detroit and Flint, Michigan, have experienced significant economic losses (and still haven't recovered), while property values in Phoenix, Arizona, and Austin, Texas, are insanely high.

Why? More people want to live in Phoenix than Detroit, which is why Detroit properties are valued significantly less. So to get a good idea of how homes are appreciating in your area, we need to get information specifically about that city and possibly even the specific neighborhood.

Real estate agents (although they are incentivized to sell you a property) are a good resource, but I prefer to look at the data. Do your real estate research on websites such as **realtor.com**, **redfin.com** and **zillow.com**—it can provide this kind of historical information.

REI Way to Wealth #2: Asset Leverage

Leverage is an investment strategy of using borrowed money—specifically, the use of various financial instruments or borrowed capital—to increase the potential return of an investment.

Leverage in real estate is to use other people's money to increase your returns without having to put as much of your own capital into it.

Real estate leverage is one of the great advantages of real estate investments over other asset classes. But it does come with risks, so make sure you understand how to use it before taking on serious debt.

Simply put, leverage in real estate is OPM—"other people's money."

Use OPM to buy your own assets—assets that generate income for you and, hopefully, appreciate with time and provide you with other benefits, as we discuss in this chapter.

Banks love to lend money for real assets such as real estate. And although banks do many things, their primary role is to take deposits—from those with money—and then make loans, lent to those who need funds. Banks are intermediaries between depositors (who lend money to the bank) and borrowers (to whom the bank lends money).

If you want to buy a rental property, you can often borrow 75% of the purchase price from a mortgage lender. You only come up with 25% of the price on your own.

Compare that to buying stocks. Brokerages don't allow nearly the same percentage. If they even let you buy on margin (taking a loan from the brokerage), they often only lend up to 50% of your portfolio balance—and at high interest rates on top of that. And even worse, they can "call" the leveraged stocks you bought on margin if the stocks go down in value. In words, they can force you to sell at a loss (aka margin call).

That doesn't happen in real estate investing. The bank isn't going to send you a "loan call" asking for their money if the market tanks—at least not as long as you're making your payments.☺

Real estate leverage helps out real estate investors by reducing the amount of cash they need to buy a property.

The median home price in America is $428,700. Imagine if you had to come up with all of that money up front just to buy one rental property. Only the super wealthy would own rentals. The good news is you don't have to be. But (cue my late-night 1990s infomercial voice) "wait, there's more!"

Here's how I (as do many other long-term wealthy investors) have leveraged my way into multi-million-dollar high-end luxury properties. I've been doing this since 2000, but recently it got a cool acronym.

The BRRRR means simply buy, renovate, rent, refinance, repeat. Depending on what you are going to do with the property, you may lose one R, but nevertheless the principles are still tried and true.

Through the BRRRR method, you'll buy a distressed or less desireable property, add value through rehab, build cash flow by renting, refinance into a better financial position—and then do the whole thing again. Over time, you'll build a real estate portfolio that's the envy of your fellow investors.

Let's break down each part of this method.

1. Buy

You have several options to buy—cash, seller financing, a hard money loan, bank loan, or a private loan. These different financing options will result in different costs—both acquisition and holding costs.

This will require an intensive deal analysis, which includes calculating the cost of renovations, estimating monthly rental expenses, and confirming that the resulting rental income will provide a sufficient profit margin. It is a critical point that determines the investment outcome.

When buying a distressed property, it's important to calculate the after-repair value (ARV). ARV is the estimated value of the home after you renovate or rehab the property. To determine ARV, you compare the final renovation of the home to similar homes that have recently sold in the area.

Keep in mind, most lenders will finance 75% of an investment property's value. If you're new to this, I would use the 70% rule to estimate the cost of repairs and after-repair value, which will help you determine a maximum offer to be made on a property.

Use this equation to apply the 70% rule to your property:

AFTER-REPAIR VALUE (ARV) ✕ .70 ─ REPAIR COST ESTIMATE =
TOP PURCHASE PRICE

Using this rule of thumb, you can better ensure that a profit margin will remain after renovating a property.

Calculating the top purchase price gives you a sense of the amount of money you should invest in the property. The only variable here is if you're renting (the typical R in BRRRR) or reselling (aka flipping)—but the rule is helpful in both cases as it relies on rehab costs and expenses.

Depending on the market you're in, the 70% rule doesn't *always* work, but until you have developed the knowledge and further understand this method, it's a great place to start. It's also good to have friends in the industry—an experienced agent, long-term lender, or a circle of investor friends—to give an estimate of what they feel the property will appraise for once it's been renovated.

But no matter what, always do the math and check your numbers!

2. Rehab/Renovate

There are two key questions to keep in mind when renovating.

1. What do I need to do to make this house livable and functional?
2. What renovations can I make that will add more value than their cost?

If you do a renovation correctly and you add value, you are pretty much guaranteed to recover your investment—plus make a return, which is the whole point.

Unless you're in the luxury market, generally speaking, "improvements" such as garage conversions, over-the-top kitchens, expensive chandeliers, and finished attics and basements aren't going to get you a high return on your money. Keep it modest and straightforward.

According to *Remodeling Magazine*'s 2022 "Cost vs. Value Report," a major kitchen remodel only recoups around 56% of the costs, significantly lower than a minor kitchen remodel, which recoups 71% of costs on average (Kalfrin and Rogacz, 2022).

It's also rarely worth putting money into luxury improvements for a rental. Instead, consider changes such as fresh paint, new flooring, new tile, new plumbing fixtures, and bright lighting. You get a big bang for your buck on these types of improvements, and your property will show better than the rest.

Make sure everything is functionable and in good working order because being a slumlord or a bargain basement flipper will cost you more money in the long run. A well-done renovation also gives you flexibility should you ever want or need to offload a property.

I intentionally look for the worst properties that need massive repairs because I know other investors, and retail buyers, will probably ignore them. The lack of demand, and the longer it sits on the market, motivates sellers to drop their prices.

One of the many times I bought the ugliest house—it wasn't just the worst on the street, but on several streets. It sat on the market for over a year! The price per square foot was much lower than any other comp in the area because it needed a massive renovation. Most people couldn't get past the fact it was stuck in 1995 and the amount of work it needed, but me—all I could see was the opportunity.

Now I don't recommend doing that for your first or second project. But since this wasn't my first rodeo, I know: **the greater the reno, the greater the reward.**

Some of the "best" problems to look for are:

- Roofs. The money spent on replacing a roof tends to come back to you through a higher appraisal. Roofing issues can scare away buyers—and lenders—which will help you get a property for less.

- Ugly kitchens. Ugly is usable, even if outdated. A kitchen partially in a demo stage makes the house ineligible for FHA financing (loans from the government for first-time home buyers) resulting in it being easier to buy with cash. This is one from a laundry list of rules on FHA qualifications. To learn more about the requirements and low down payment and interest rate of the FHA program, go to **www.fha.com**.

- Nasty bathrooms. Most bathrooms aren't huge, so it doesn't take much in material and labor to update them. Updating bathrooms is typically an easy fix and will result in a higher ARV.

- Wall issues. Drywall damage can also make a property ineligible for financing, but drywall is fairly simple and easy to repair.

- Overgrown landscaping. Out of control shrubs, trees, and other vegetation frightens buyers, but costs very little to fix. You don't need a company or a permit to do landscaping, so it doesn't take much to improve and will pay dividends on your curb appeal.

Targeting properties where you can make these types of repairs—and you can snag for below market value—can add equity to your deals and result in more cash in your pocket.

3. Rent

Banks rarely want to refinance a rental property that isn't occupied, so getting a tenant is a good first step.

It's critical to diligently screen applicants so you get good tenants who pay every month. This also helps you when you go to finance. While bank appraisers shouldn't put too much value on how clean and well-kept the property is, everyone is human, and first impressions do make a difference.

4. Refinance

If you don't have a relationship with a bank or a lender, here are two things you will need to ask:

1. Do they offer cash-out refis, or do they only pay off debt? If they don't offer cash-out refis—move on. Cash-out refinancing is key in this method. Cash-out refi is when you replace your current mortgage with a new one that has a larger outstanding principal balance, and you get the difference in a lump sum of cash. You get back the cash you put into the property *plus* you get tax-free money from the increase of appreciation you built into the property because of the value you added.

2. What "seasoning period" do they require? This is how long you have to own a property before the bank lends on the appraised value instead of how much you've invested. Sometimes lenders want the property to "season" for 6 to 12 months before refinancing. Instead, look for lenders who are willing to lend on the appraised value as soon as a property has been renovated and rented.

To find the best banks, ask other investors you know. Websites such as ListSource (www.listsource.com) or CoreLogic (www.corelogic.com) let you search for every loan made to non-owner occupants in your city and price range in the last year. This search will cost a couple of hundred dollars, but it's money well spent because it saves you *time*. Buying time by acquiring knowledge so you can move quickly is *always* a good investment.

5. Repeat

Now that you've done it once, you rinse and repeat. Take everything you learned, see what went well and what could have gone better. Find areas to improve upon, and use that knowledge to do even better on the next one.

And just like in business, processes and systems help you accomplish everything faster and will cut down on mistakes—and stress. The better documented your processes are, the less you'll have to worry about missing something.

BRRRR in Real-Life

So here's a real-life example of how I stumbled onto this process and have used it over and over again throughout the last two decades, long before the acronym BRRRR was ever created.

Rewind to 2001 and the Stone House (I always name my properties to keep them straight), a 4 bedroom, 1 bath house located in a small town in western Pennsylvania.

I picked up the Stone House in a bank foreclosure for a whopping $23,000. Houses in that area and similar in size to the one I bought were selling between $82,000 and $85,000. I also did a comp on rent in the area, and houses of that size were renting for $700–$800/month—with very few available, let alone nice ones to choose from.

Now, this house needed work. It was 80+ years old and hadn't been updated in 40 years. The floor joists were cracked. The kitchen was small with brown and white linoleum floors and yellow appliances. The bedrooms had wood paneling. The bathroom was so tiny you could be on the toilet yet reach the tub faucet to turn it on! But the glaring problem was the house had settled so much there was a 2-inch slope you could actually feel when walking through the house. Imagine putting a marble on your floor, and it quickly runs back to the corner of your kitchen with speed, every time. Congrats! You just bought a major issue.

This was a massive reno project. And it was only my second one at this point.

I had a new roof put on, new siding, and updated all the flooring. I created a new kitchen layout with all new cabinets, opened up a closet to make the bathroom bigger, replaced all those floor joists, and put a jack stud in the basement to raise the house a ¼-inch every week (to get that 2-inch slope out).

I shopped prices and found good yet reasonable contractors for the major items, plus my dad helped, and I did what I could. My all-in renovation cost was $18,000 (remember this was 20+ years ago).

Here's how the numbers work. Stick with me. I promise you that this one principle, when leveraged properly, will change your financial future.

House bought with "cash": $23,000 [$13,000 of my own money + $10,000 line of credit (OPM)].

Cost of renovation: $18,000 paid with line of credit (OPM).

After the renovation was complete, I did a cash-out refi on the property (OPM).

With the appraisal value of $120,000, the cash out refi gave me $96,000. I paid the $28,000 line of credit off, which left me with $68,000!

But remember, I only had $13,000 of my own money into it!

The house then rented for $750/month (cash flow).

After a couple of years, I realized I personally didn't like being a landlord, but I loved flipping. Although I received $14,000 in cash flow from rent, I sold the house later for $129,000 (property appreciation).

This isn't a traditional BRRRR method because I sold the house after a couple of years, but let's run through the math and see what my initial $13,000 turned into:

$13,000 of my own money + $28,000 from an LOC. The appraisal came in at $120,000. The bank gave me $96,000 on a cash-out refi. After paying off the line of credit, I was left with $68,000:	$68,000
I then sold the property for $129,000. Paid off the $96,000 refi mortgage on it. After closing fees, I was left with another $24,000:	$24,000
That is:	$92,000!

But we aren't even done yet.

We didn't even factor in the rent collected! Once you add everything up, it's approximately $106,000 in total! All made on my initial $13,000 investment.

If you put profits from the sale of a property into a separate escrowed bank account to use the section 1031 exchange, these can be *tax-free* (see more in Chapter 13). You have six months to find another real estate property to buy and avoid paying taxes on your profits from the sale.

> **Rather than having a hobby that *takes* from you, find a hobby that *adds* to you.**

Now some people would say I should have held onto that house because I would have made even more, and they aren't wrong. However, you get to choose what type of investor you are. Real estate investing was, and still is, something I love to do. Some successful people choose to golf or go on shopping trips. But I love this. The bigger the project, the more difficult the renovation, the more moving parts—the more I love it.

Here's how I look at it: Does this give me the opportunity to add to my health, add to my wealth, bring me more joy, or give me an opportunity to contribute? If it doesn't do one of those four things, then I don't have time for it.

REI Way to Wealth #3: Tax Advantages and Savings

Another big financial perk are the tax deductions you can take for real estate investments. I talk about taxes in depth in Chapter 12 but want to cover some real estate specific ones here. And since we only retain a small percentage of what we hear, or read, if you see this twice, it has a better chance of sticking.

Direct expenses that you incur for property management and maintenance are deductible. These include:

- Related taxes and insurance;
- Interest on your mortgage;
- Fees paid for property management;
- Building maintenance;
- Repairs to the building.

You can also write off typical business expenses, just as with any other business. Qualified real estate investment business expenses may include:

- Advertising and marketing;
- Office space and supplies;
- Business equipment (e.g. computer, tablets);
- Legal and accounting fees;
- Travel and meals;
- Gas and vehicle expenses.

Because these deductions reduce taxable income, you save money and can keep more of what you make (see Chapter 12 for a refresher).

Suppose that rental income from your real estate business is $40,000, and that you have qualified expenses of $9,000. When you deduct expenses on your taxes, the taxable income drops to $31,000.

As I've shared in other chapters, make sure you have a properly detailed accounting of your expenses by keeping receipts and other records that verify and can substantiate the expenses you claim.

Depreciate Costs over Time

This is one of the best parts of being a real estate investor. Depreciation is a *phantom expense*. It's a deduction you get to take, without it having to come out of your own checkbook to buy (like all other deductions). To take a tax deduction, you have to *spend* money—an investment into your business—so you get to take the deduction. But not with depreciation. Depreciation denotes minimal loss in the asset's value, usually due to wear and tear.

For example, if you're an investor who holds real estate that produces rental income, property depreciation becomes an expense to claim on your taxes. This deduction helps reduce your taxable income which results in less taxes you have to pay. Deductions for depreciation are taken each year for the property's life expectancy. At this time, the IRS sets residential property life expectancy at 27.5 years and commercial property life expectancy at 39 years.

Suppose that you buy a rental property where just the building's value (no land) is $350,000. When you split that value into yearly chunks (for each of the 27.5 years), you see that your deduction is $12,727 for the property's depreciation. This deduction is called a phantom expense because unlike all other deductions, you're not spending *more* to pay less in taxes.

However, after you sell the property, the standard income tax rate takes affect for the claimed depreciation. This is a tax formulated to get back some of the deducted depreciation, but you might look at other tax strategies, such as a 1031 exchange or an opportunity zone investment—to help alleviate this tax. (More on that in a minute.)

Use a Pass-through Deduction

When you own rental property as a pass-through entity (such as a sole proprietorship, a partnership, or an LLC or S corp), the rental income collected becomes qualified business income (QBI) according to real estate tax law. As a pass-through, you can deduct up to 20% of the QBI on your personal taxes.

Suppose that your LLC owns a building complex and your rental income totals $30,000 each year. When you use a pass-through deduction, you can deduct a maximum of $6,000 on your personal tax return. Remember that all deductions and tax strategies come with rules and regulations that you must follow. This particular perk and other parts of the Tax Cut and Jobs Act is expected to expire in 2025.

Understanding Capital Gains

When you sell as asset such as property for profit, you may be assessed a capital gains tax. Be aware that there are two types of capital gains: short term and long term. If you plan to invest in real estate or start a real estate business, you want to know about these.

I had an expensive lesson learning this one. In my early 20s, I started doing more flips than holds and couldn't figure out why I was getting nailed with taxes. Simply put, if you are keeping properties for less than a year, you're paying taxes just like earned income. It's only when you keep properties for more than a year that you get some savings. Let me share with you what I wish I had known about a lot sooner: the difference between short-term and long-term capital gains.

Short-Term Capital Gains   You realize a short-term capital gain when you profit from selling an asset within a year of owning it. This situation can have a negative effect on your taxes because the short-term gain can be taxed as *ordinary income*.

Consider this example:

You earn $100,000 from your 9-to-5 day job or your business.

You sell a property you purchased for investment only six months after the date of purchase. You make a $100,000 profit on this sale. When added to your day job income, your profit essentially doubles your income for tax purposes because now you brought in $200,000.

Depending on how you file your taxes, additional income may push you into the next tax bracket. In this situation, you can end up paying a larger tax bill at a percentage rate higher than you expected.

Long-Term Capital Gains   You realize a long-term capital gain on the profit from selling a property when you have held that asset for a year or longer.

If you can wait 12 months to sell, until the anniversary of your purchase (plus one day just to be sure), you will keep more of your profit. Why?

Because long-term capital gains incur a much lower tax rate than your standard ordinary "earned" income.

As a bonus: Depending on the amount of your income, you may not have to pay *any* capital gains tax. Suppose that you and your spouse make $74,000 per year combined and file your taxes jointly. Your long-term capital gains are tax-free because the tax rate for your income level is 0%. In that case, you keep every cent of the profit you make when selling a property. This is a great way to get some significant savings when selling assets and why you may want to consider holding them a little longer.

Deferring Taxes

Again, something I wish I knew a lot sooner. There are a few ways the government helps incentivize investors, and deferring taxes is one of them. If I had this book

20+ years ago, I would have saved hundreds of thousands of dollars by doing this a lot sooner. The 1031 exchange is a great tool for deferring taxes.

1031 Exchange   As a real estate investing tool, the 1031 exchange allows investors to swap one investment property for another. In this way, they can defer capital gains (or losses) or capital gains taxes that they would have had to pay at the time of a sale.

The five main rules to qualify for a 1031 exchange are:

- It must be a like-kind property;
- It can be an investment or business property only (cannot be primary residence);
- The replacement property should be of equal or greater value to the one being sold;
- The replacement property must be identified within 45 days;
- The replacement property must be purchased within 180 days.

If all rules are met, an investor may defer the capital gains tax payment due on the sale of the initial property. However, you have to set up the exchange properly to use it. There are rules and requirements, and these depend on circumstances such as the timing of your buying and selling transactions. Following the 1031 exchange program can be complicated, and consulting with a qualified tax strategist is always recommended.

Remember: You can use the 1031 exchange to defer now, but any tax you owed becomes due when you eventually take the profits from your transactions.

Opportunity Zones   An Opportunity Zone is a community nominated by the state and certified by the US Treasury Department as qualifying for this program. There are approximately 8,700 Opportunity Zones in all 50 states, Washington, DC, and US territories. A list can be found at the US Department of Housing and Urban Development website.

You can think of Opportunity Zones as tracts of land that serve a low-income community or are considered disadvantaged. The 2017 Tax Cuts and Jobs Act offers tax breaks to those who invest their money for development and economic stimulation of Opportunity Zones.

Here's how these tax credits can work for you:

1. Find a group of investors to work with and put any unrealized capital gains you have into a Qualified Opportunity Fund.
2. Help direct the money from the Qualified Opportunity Fund into improving the property located at the Opportunity Zone selected.

3. Make sure to follow the program rules. When you do, you can receive tax advantages such as:

- You can defer paying capital gains until 2026. But if you sell your piece of the Qualified Opportunity Fund before 2026, you pay the capital gains tax at that time.
- You can even avoid paying capital gains by keeping your money in the fund for at least 10 years.

Saving on FICA Tax (aka self-employment tax)   This last tax advantage is how you can save on self-employment taxes. Self-employment tax adds up because anyone who is self-employed must pay both portions of the FICA tax, consisting of Social Security and Medicare, for the employer and the employee.

If you own rental property, the income you receive isn't classified as *earned income*. And because of that fact, one of the taxes you are able to avoid as a real estate investor is FICA tax (aka payroll tax).

Let's break down the numbers:

Suppose you are a consultant who brings in $60,000 per year. That money is *earned income*, and you owe self-employment taxes at a 15.3% tax rate, which means your dishing out about $9,180. Now suppose that the rental property you own produces $60,000 a year in rental income. Because that money is *passive income*, you get to keep that money in your pocket.

REI Way to Wealth #4: Flexibility

Whether it was the savings and loan crisis of the 1980s and 90s, the 2008–2009 financial crisis, or the COVID-19 pandemic in 2020 and 2021, those who take advantage of market disruption all have a common characteristic: flexibility.

Successful real estate returns have favored those with flexibility. In an environment where the market can shift rapidly and restrictions can inhibit an investment's performance, those who are willing to embrace flexibility as an investor mindset and those who view real estate like I do—as having the ultimate flexibility—will receive greater reward on any type of risk.

For instance, an investor willing to invest in both multifamily and retail has an advantage in acquiring mixed-use projects over investors with narrow mindsets who focus on just one. In real estate investing, not only does the investor with a flexible mindset have a huge advantage, but real estate in general has massive flexibility.

Let's say, for example, you get into a single-family home and you want to live there. But something changes in your personal finances and you can no longer afford the house. Are you living in an area where the house would rent for more than you're paying for the mortgage? Is it in an area where Airbnb or a short-term rental would maximize your profit dollars?

Certain properties have restrictions on zoning, HOAs, and other types of covenants, but if you look at flexibility as a key factor when purchasing real estate, it is a lot harder to lose, unlike buying a stock where you are just betting on the stock to win.

In many other markets, there are currents of corruption, technology change, and competition, but with real estate people always need somewhere to live, whether that is buying or renting a property. As long as you are not over-leveraged, even if the market turns, you have the ability to navigate as the market shifts.

Change in any market is inevitable, and once you understand economic cycles, you start to see patterns and know which are going to repeat approximately when.

Investors respond to change in the markets two ways:

1. **Fear it:**

    Refuse to change, miss out on the opportunities that come your way, watch your profits shrink, and eventually lose money.

2. **Figure it out:**

    Embrace it, modify your investment strategy, and reap the benefits from the opportunities that just presented themselves.

Successful investors understand that to succeed, they must be prepared and take advantage of opportunities that come their way. This could be during an upswing or a downswing as no market ever continues forever.

If you're in an up market, guess what. Winter is coming at some point. If you're in a down market or in the midst of an economic financial downturn, the same applies. It's not going to last forever.

Economies and markets work in cycles—expansion, peak, recession, recovery—then rinse and repeat. It's the economic version of BRRRR.

When you look at the historic list of expansions as well as economic recessions, recoveries, and big booms in the market, you see this exact pattern over and over again.

Flexibility in real estate is the key function to surviving downturns.

REI Way to Wealth #5: Cash Flow

These are the two magic words to any real estate investor—*cash flow*.

According to Roofstock.com, "cash flow is the amount of profit you have each month after collecting all income, paying all operating expenses, and setting aside cash reserves for future repairs. For buy-and-hold real estate investors, cash flow is the primary lever used to increase income" (Jahnke, 2022).

Cash flow compares income and expenses incurred in connection with a rented property. If the income exceeds the expenses, it is **positive** cash flow. If the expenses are greater than the income, the cash flow is **negative**.

Most real estate investors can estimate the gross rental income for a property. But it's the actual cost of owning and operating their rental that people don't anticipate.

You can get your pretax cash flow by taking the total of your annual rent and deducting all the expenses, such as the mortgage payments, insurance, and property taxes.

Basically, the expenses can be divided into:

- **Purchase costs** – transfer tax as well as notary and registry costs;
- **Loan costs** – debt service (interest and repayment);
- **Maintenance costs** – reserves for maintenance;
- **Management costs.**

Four Important Ratios Every Real Estate Investor Needs to Know

I don't want to tell you *how* to build a house without giving you all the tools to make it as easy as possible—giving you the greatest chance of success—so here are a few more tools from the toolbox, things that will help you understand the REI world even more.

1. **Capitalization Rate** (Cap Rate)

    Cap rate can be an important factor when analyzing an investment property. It is used to measure what the possible return will be on any given property. It also provides insight into whether the property will give you a good return for your money.

    Here is the formula.

First, you'll need to figure the Net Operating Income (NOI) which is similar to net profit for a business. Add up all the revenue the property will collect and then subtract all the expenses the property will have.

You then divide that number by the property's market value (or you can use the purchase price; investors will use one or both).

Here's an example: If your property has a current value of $500,000 and your NOI is $50,000, the result when you divide is .10. Once you convert that to a percentage, you get 10%.

Generally speaking, investors look for a cap rate of 5% to 10%.

And although it can be a quick tool to assess an investment, it should not be used alone. There are variables that can affect the cap rate location of the property and other factors.

Bottom line: The capitalization rate can be super helpful to compare properties.

2. Cash-on-Cash Return

Cash on cash return is what you can expect to receive on the money you invest in your real estate property. It's an important formula because it will show you how much money you are likely to earn off of the money you invest and takes into account mortgage payments and interest paid to banks or other lenders.

To calculate your total amount of money invested, you will want to take the total purchase price plus any closing costs, subtract any mortgage on the property, and add any upgrades being made to the property to increase total value. Your upgrade list can include things such as replacing the air conditioner, upgrading the wiring, or adding tile flooring or new appliances.

Although there is no perfect number, generally speaking most investors are looking for a cash on cash return that's higher than 8%. There are some who won't touch a deal for less than double digit returns and others who are fine with less than 8% (depending on the market they're in).

3. Return on Investment (ROI)

ROI, on any investment, is important to measure. It helps evaluate how much money or profit, you have earned on an investment as a percentage of its total cost.

The cost method calculates ROI by dividing the investment gain in a property by that property's costs.

Here's an example. Let's say you purchased a property for $200,000 in cash. After its renovation, which cost $50,000, the property's value is now $300,000. This makes your gain $50,000.

To use the cost method, divide the gain by all the costs related to the purchase, repairs, and rehabilitation of the property.

The ROI in this example is $50,000 ÷ $250,000 = 20%.

There is another way many real estate investors use for calculating ROI, which is called the out-of-pocket. This is commonly used when you put your own cash into the property for a down payment and then get a mortgage for the rest.

Let's say your out-of-pocket cash is $50,000 plus you have to put in $50,000 more for renovation, giving you a total of $100,000 cash in. With a new property value of $300,000, your potential profit is $200,000.

Your ROI in this case is $200,000 ÷ $300,000 = 66%. It's a huge difference because, when you use leverage (remember, when we talked about other people's money—OPM), you can increase your ROI and use less of your own money.

Remember that real estate ROI typically varies by *risk*—the more risk, the higher the ROI. Many people settle for lower ROIs to sleep better at night. Just remember that historically the S&P 500 annual return is 9.3%, so you may want to keep that in mind when deciding what type of returns you want to shoot for.

4. **Loan-to-Value Ratio (LTV)**

If you want to invest in real estate, this is a good ratio to be familiar with because LTVs are not just used by investors, but they are also used by banks and any lending institution looking to give you a loan (including refis).

Let's say a property is being sold for $400,000 and an independent appraiser for the bank gives it a $375,000 value. This appraisal is critical in obtaining a loan since most lenders will only lend up to 80% LTV for owner occupied properties and 75% LTV for investment properties. If either appraises for less than the purchase price you're about to pay, you'd need to make up the difference or go back to the seller to renegotiate new terms.

This will help you do an analysis on the property to know where you stand before purchasing. It's important to know that these benchmarks only apply to the first year.

As time goes on, your equity in the property will increase, inflation will cause your operating expenses and property taxes to increase. All of these variables will change the ratios, so it's important to stay on top of the data and see how the market is heading to have the best handle on your investment for the future.

The 1% and 50% Rule

Analyzing deals is crucial to the success of any real estate investor, so here's a quick tool to help. Applying certain rules can help quickly determine whether a real estate investment is likely to be profitable.

The 1% Rule   When investing in real estate, you can use the 1% rule to evaluate the cost of the property you're investing in against the total revenue you expect it to provide.

Before a real estate holding can pass the 1%-rule measure, the rent received each month must be equivalent to or more than 1% of the cost of the purchase (Nowacki, 2022).

If your total cost to acquire the property is $500,000 and you are planning on receiving rent of $5,000 a month, that is 1%. When you are looking at buying a rental property of any kind, this rule is a quick way to evaluate it—since 1% is generally good for many investors.

Investors can use the 1% rule for two purposes:

- Evaluating a property's potential for profit before buying it;
- As a guideline for how much rent should be charged.

Consider the 1% rule as a guideline, but understand that it may not apply in some cases or in certain markets.

The 50% Rule   The 50% rule is used to determined the property's expenses and profitability. It was designed to help those looking to invest because one of the most common mistakes investors make is estimating their profits too high and their real expenses far too low.

Here it is in action.

Let's say you buy a rental property that generates $100,000 in annual gross revenue. When using the 50% rule, $50,000 of that would be your operating expenses for the property, and the other $50,000 would be your net income.

Continuing to examine the 50% rule of real estate investing, consider what expenses the 50% applies to and what it doesn't. The main thing to remember is that it doesn't factor in any of your mortgage payments, interest on loans, or any fees such as property management or HOAs.

Calculating the expense portion of the 50% rule includes expenses such as taxes, insurance, repairs, and maintenance, as well as factoring in utilities and any vacancy losses. Of course, if you pay cash for a property and perform the management duties allow yourself, you avoid those expenses. And bonus if there's no HOA, too.

To calculate the 50% rule for vetting a real estate transaction, start by estimating the gross rent—monthly or annually—and then divide by two. The scenario may look something like this:

- You expect $4000 per month in rent; apply the 50% rule and factor $2000 for expenses.

- Add together your mortgage payment ($1,400), HOA fees ($150), and property management fees ($0 since you're self-managed); that sum is $1,550.
- Subtract this sum from the 50% of the rent that's not set aside, and you have cash of $450 left over (monthly). That's your cash flow.

You can use the 50% rule for real estate investments as a guideline for evaluating profitability for a potential property you're considering. Like any guideline, there are situations where it simply won't work well in that given scenario. But the rule is a great place to start for helping an investor understand the numbers and avoid underestimating their costs.

Of course, there are many things to consider beyond this. You'll want to think about costs over time, and projected increases for taxes, property wear and tear, and insurances. How will these increases in expenses compare with increases in rent? Things like inflation can certainly benefit investors with rental properties because they can charge more in rent, but it can also drive housing prices way up, making it cost more to acquire the same properties.

But, as always, do your research. Check out the rental market in the area surrounding the potential investment property. Find out about rental pricing trends and the level of demand for rentals, and evaluate the area's overall desirability. Look at property values in the area, get estimates for insurance coverage, and find out about associated utility costs to help determine what your actual costs might be.

Use your additional research to add substance to the quick calculations you've performed based on the 1% and 50% rules. Your efforts will pay off through more informed decision-making about your potential property investment.

These ratios aside, the REI hat trick coupled with the five ways you make money in real estate, can you see why I'm not only passionate about this kind of investing but more importantly why it's undeniably a *wealth habit*? There are countless ways you can use real estate to advance wealth. No other area of financial life allows you to use leverage so easily, cheaply, and (relatively) safely. Along with owning a business, real estate investing is one of the main ways that Americans become wealthy. Are you going to be next?

CHAPTER 18

Recession-Proof Your Finances— and Your Life

I t's mid-2022 as I write this, and everybody's talking about a recession. But nobody's telling you exactly what you need to do to make sure you don't take a financial hit during such a difficult time.

First and foremost, don't make irrational moves based on fear.

If you react before thinking through and planning your next financial move, you could actually make things worse and not better.

No market will go up forever. So you always have to be preparing for the winter time in any market that you're in.

Look at the various dips in the market over the last 30 years. Depending on the year you were in, it could have felt disastrous, but when you pull back over the course of time, you see that the times of winter end too.

I was just two years into my first business when the 9/11 attacks happened. Just seven years later, as I was heavier into real estate investing, the 2008 crash happened.

In 2020, when covid swept across the entire world, I just finished some short-term real estate projects—then travel stopped on a dime.

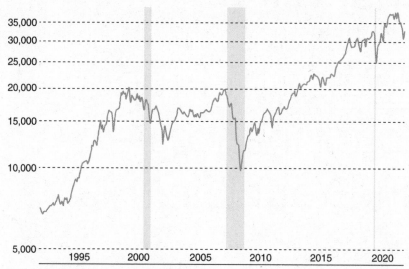

Source: Macrotrends LLC, Dow Jones - DJIA - 100 Year Historical Chart. https://www.macrotrends
.net/1319/dow-jones-100-year-historical-chart - last accessed by Aug 17, 2022.

Recessions and market downturns can be challenging, but the greatest threat to your own personal economy is lack of financial literacy.

The 2020 pandemic-induced financial disaster lasted for months. Although some industries saw immense challenges, others had massive increases—and more billionaires were created during that time than any other in history. Why?

Well, before we dive into that, let's break down what a recession is and what it can mean to you.

A recession by definition is a "significant decline in general economic activity."

This sounds scary, but it just means that anytime our country has two consecutive quarters of a decline reflected by the gross domestic product (GDP) and other indicators such as unemployment, it's declared a recession. So when the National Bureau of Economic Research—basically our government—sees a significant decline in economic activity that lasts more than just a few months, whether it's the GDP, real income, unemployment, wholesale, retail sales, or production—they're going to call it a recession.

So what does that mean for *you*?

There are a lot of things you can do to financially prepare for a recession.

What few realize is during times of recession, people who understand the principles of this book, who have a high level of wealth, net worth, or financial intelligence, they become *more* wealthy.

Why? Because they already have developed the *wealth habits* to not only protect themselves ahead of any potential economic downturn, they also are perfectly leveraged and positioned to capitalize on what's coming. And that's why and how more billionaires were created in the early stages of the pandemic.

The reality is you can't control the markets, but there are some things you can do to reduce the impact of an economic downturn.

A good place to start is with the following six things:

1. Remember, there are always opportunities;
2. High-yield savings accounts and CDs;
3. Minimize expenses and spending;
4. Consider recession-proof stocks;
5. Look at recession-proof businesses;
6. Invest in treasuries.

Let's break down each of these.

Remember, There Is *Always* an Opportunity

You always get what you focus on. Focus on the problem, and you'll find more. Focus on finding solutions, and you'll find an opportunity. (See Chapter 3 for a refresher on solution-based thinking.)

For example, when cash or lending dries up, or people lose their homes during an economic downturn, what do they need to do? They need to go and rent.

There will be an influx of people who need to rent as opposed to those who have enough liquid cash to go out and buy their dream home. When you're looking for investments, look for rental properties—duplexes, triplexes, quads, large apartment buildings, townhomes, or even land to develop. These can be great investments during a recession.

High-Yield Savings Accounts and CDs

You will hardly get any return, but it is a very safe place to stash cash. It also is a great place to keep your emergency fund, the only money you ever want liquid, and not leveraged, in an asset. Having a solid emergency fund (as we discussed in Chapter 15) is crucial to long-term financial success and protection.

Credit availability tends to dry up quickly in times of financial difficulty, downturns in the market, or if a recession hits. If necessary, use your emergency fund to cover critical expenses, but keep your budget tight on discretionary spending to make that emergency fund last.

Minimize Living Expenses and Spending

Take a deeper look into your living expenses and monthly budget.

If you make it a habit to live within your means each and every day during the good times, you are less likely to go into debt when gas or food prices go up.

If you have a spouse or are a two-income family, see how close you can get to living off only one income. It will carry you through during the bad times, but in good economic times, this tactic will allow you to save incredible amounts of money (The Investopedia Team, 2022). Imagine how quickly you could buy another investment property, add to your investment portfolio, and retire much earlier if you had an extra $40,000 or $50,000 a year to invest.

This is also why one of the *wealth habits* is multiple income streams. Check out Chapter 6 for a refresher.

If you don't have all of your money in one place, your losses should be mitigated, making it easier to ride out the dips in the market.

In particular, build a portfolio of investment pairs that aren't strongly correlated—meaning that when one is up, the other is down, and vice versa—such as stocks and bonds.

This also means you should consider asset classes and stocks in businesses that are unrelated to your primary occupation, business, or income stream (The Investopedia team, 2022).

Recession-Proof Stocks

When the news is all about the stock market tanking, it might have you wondering if you should pull back or get out. But don't stop investing because the stock market is down. Historically, bear times don't last.

All the experts say that in the long run, slow and steady stock-buying easily beats trying to time market dips. So based on the data, and having gone through several economic pullbacks and downturns, here are some of the stocks I look at:

- Big Pharma stocks can be an ideal recession-proof investment. And it is proven that during financially difficult times, mental health prescription drugs are at an all-time high.
- Again, when money starts to dry up, everybody wants to save and luxuries or optional spending for the low-income and middle classes almost stop. Where are they going to buy things when people are trying to save money? Discount retailers. Think Walmart.
- Other examples of recession-proof industries are alcohol and utilities.

In terms of investing, being prepared for a recession involves taking a long-term approach to your investment goals. Be realistic about your risk tolerance and maintain a diversified portfolio.

Look at Recession-Proof Businesses

There's no such thing as a recession-proof business, since every financial crisis is different. But certain types of businesses are better able to survive tough economic times.

The key is finding a business, and a business model, that's resilient: things such as laundromats, storage facilities, RV parks, trailer parks, landfills, waste management, funeral homes, handyman and home repair services (HVAC, electric, etc.), towing, and auto repair services.

Think about necessity businesses over luxury, or "optional," businesses such as grocery stores. People still need to eat. When they are thinking about going on a luxury vacation or buy a bigger home, they may skip those in a recession. But you know they're going to eat. Grocery stores are always a great recession-proof investment.

Recession-proof businesses are simple tried-and-true businesses that have withstood the test of time. They are long-standing businesses. They have very weak or poor competition. They have a very simplistic business model yet are still needed in the marketplace. They have minimal innovation. And they are often considered "boring," yet boring is as close to recession-proof as you can get.

Remember, boring can still make you rich—not to mention being a perfect investment in an economic downturn. You can search for businesses for sale at websites such as **www.bizbuysell.com**.

Some other types of business that don't see much decline in difficult times are in industries such as home improvement stores, skilled trades contractors, online marketing agencies, e-commerce stores with low-price items, hair

> **Your mindset, ability to adapt, speed of decisions, and willingness to change will be the four keys to your success in any market, any business, or any economy.**

salons, funeral homes, legal services, online software companies, and real estate holding/investment companies.

If you decide to start a business or venture into another industry to diversify your income during economic uncertainty, you'll need to learn how to manage it, and yourself, under extra pressure.

Treasuries

Examples of recession-proof assets include gold, silver, and US Treasury bonds. Several types of bond funds are particularly popular with risk-averse investors.

Treasuries are debt obligations issued and backed by the full faith and credit of the US government.

The primary goal of a bond fund is often that of generating monthly income for investors. It is also referred to as a debt fund. A pooled investment vehicle that invests primarily in bonds (government or corporate) and other debt instruments, such as MBS (mortgage-backed securities) is another option.

While bond funds and other conservative investments have shown be to safe havens during tough times, you also must understand that the safer an investment seems, the less growth you can expect.

Funds made up of US Treasury bonds lead the pack, as they are considered to be one of the safest because the government's ability to levy taxes and print money virtually eliminates the risk of default and provides principal protection (Hayes, 2022).

These are all important tools that are going to get you through any difficult patch in the economy so you'll come out on the other side in one piece, financially.

Eventually, economic uncertainty will settle. Being ready for change also means you need to be ready to acknowledge when things start changing for the better.

But I also mentioned billionaires at the beginning of this chapter. So why was there a new billionaire created every 30 hours during the pandemic?

In early 2020, the world counted 2,095 billionaires. Today—just over two years later—there are 2,668.

The overall wealth of billionaires grew as much in the two years (2020 to 2022) as it did in the previous 23 years! Billionaires now account for about

14% of the global GDP, which is quite a contrast to just 20 years ago when they only accounted for 4% of it.

And guess what industries grew the most. The same ones I mentioned above. The same ones *you* need to look at during the next economic challenge—energy, food, and the pharmaceutical industry.

Corporate profit and individual wealth grew the most in what areas over the last two years? Yep—energy, food, and the pharmaceutical industry.

Altogether, there are now 26 *more* billionaires primarily in the food business than there were before the 2020 pandemic. But that's for a whole other book. Right now, I want you thinking about recession-proof stocks.

The pharmaceutical industry also created several new billionaires, mostly profiting directly from covid. Moderna, for instance, has made $12 billion so far from its covid vaccine, and four individuals became billionaires thanks to profits from the vaccine (which, by the way, was developed thanks to $10 billion in US government funding paid for by the taxpayers). So let that sink in. And while it does, I'm going to leave that alone and end here.

For anyone who desires financial security and ultimately financial freedom—creating *wealth habits* is no longer a luxury, it's a *necessity*. Especially during economic downturns or recessions.

Having an **emergency fund, building strong credit, having multiple income streams, diversifying your investments, and minimizing living expenses** are critical to protect against economic and industry cycles. Most importantly, it will help you prevail during any financially difficult times.

These *wealth habits* are how the wealthy become—and *stay*—wealthy. When not applied, you run the financial risks that come from relying on the habits most Americans have built and that keep them on a perpetual hamster wheel and, ultimately, broke.

The good news is staying away from those broke habits is not magic, and it's not even complicated.

Start applying the *wealth habits* in your life, and join the movement of creating true financial freedom.

WEALTH HABIT 6

Giving Your Way to Wealth

CHAPTER 19

Contribution: Where True Wealth Lies

The Final Habit

I was 25, and I had just bought a commercial building. This didn't seem like a big deal to me—as I had bought other properties before this—but to others it seemed odd that my goal was to buy the whole street. This particular building was on the corner, so I figured if I secured the corners, it would be easier to buy the others in between.

I bought the building without a clear plan on what to do with it. I knew it was a good deal and also knew I'd figure it out. Fast-forward to a year later—it was still sitting there, empty.

One night after a long day of work I decided to call it quits and head home. I locked up my office, got into my black Escalade, and started the drive. I stopped at a red light—right on the corner by that building I owned. I remembered sitting at the light thinking, "What am I going to do with that building?"

I had an Escalade. I had a convertible. I had designer bags and fancy shoes. I had rental properties. I lived in a nice house. I traveled to beautiful places. The business I started was successful. I was in the process of creating my own line of products. I had new spa locations mapped out and was ready to buy more buildings so I could expand into three new cities. I was in talks with attorneys about franchising the spa and was making more money than most people I knew at that time, and had checked off every goal I had made to achieve "before I turned 30"—but something still felt off.

It was almost as if I was sitting at that red light, in a matter of one second, I realized everything I had and simultaneously acknowledged everything I was missing.

And as I looked at that building, I glanced up the street to the other buildings I owned. I thought to myself, "How could I create all of this, how could I climb mountain after mountain to get to *this* place and still not feel fulfilled?"

My eyes drifted back to the empty building on the corner. This time I took a deep breath and said to myself out loud, "What am I going to do with that building?" And the next thing that happened is something I've only experienced twice in my life—and something I don't talk much about because I can't really explain it—but it was as if a voice as audible as if you and I were talking answered that question and said, "Put *your* animal shelter there."

And with those five words, something clicked inside me.

I literally glanced over my shoulder into the empty back seat of my car thinking, "Did I just hear that?" The light turned green.

"Put your animal shelter there." *Your*?

Here's the thing, I never consciously thought about opening an animal shelter. I mean, yes, I wanted to save all the animals when I was a kid. And yes, I always donated to every animal-related charity and cause that sent a donation request in the mail.

But I was about to create a bigger empire. More locations, more properties, more employees, more businesses—where on earth did this come from?

Growing up, I had a children's checking account from our local bank— the bank called it a MoolaMoola account. I would send checks from my account—$5 a month to save the pandas with the World Wildlife Fund, $10 for the elephants, another $10 to the dogs. As an adult, I volunteered for organizations, attended fundraisers and charity events, and even chaired a black-tie gala for our local shelter when I was 22. But I was so focused on business and investing that I didn't really think much more of it.

I've always had empathy for abused, abandoned animals but was never allowed to have any of my own—"No animals in the house" my mom would say. So aside from a few cats and rabbits that had to live outside, I didn't really have any pets of my own as a child.

One day when I was about seven years old, in the second grade, Janice, my school bus driver, dropped me off at my dad's garage just as she did every day after school. I made my normal visit with Stella and Al at the parts store and then started to walk down to the garage.

As I took my first few steps down the hill, a copper-colored dog with short legs, matted fur, and a red collar was standing by the gate looking at me. "Woof, woof," she let out a couple barks.

I had never seen this dog before. She wasn't ours and wasn't on a leash, so I was a tad confused and maybe even a little scared because I had to walk past her. I remembered I had half a hoagie leftover from my lunch that day, so I slowly grabbed it out of my backpack and offered it to her. She devoured it. I reached out my hand to scratch her head—her tail started to wag. I pet her some more, and then we walked down to the garage, together.

"Whose dog is this?" I asked my dad, secretly wishing he'd say, "Yours."

"I don't know," he said. "She just showed up."

My parents asked around, but nobody knew whose dog she was. We ran a "Lost dog" ad in the local paper, and I was relieved when no one called to claim her.

"Can we keep her?" I asked.

"Just until we find her owner. And she can't come to the house, she has to stay here at the garage," my parents said.

Realizing that's all I was going to get—and knowing I was at the garage every day anyway—I just was excited to finally have a dog.

And my prayers were answered. Weeks went by, and no one claimed her. I named her Harley.

Only just weeks after, a tragic accident happened. My dad always had to move cars and trucks around the lot—bringing new ones in and moving others out that were done being repaired. He wasn't used to having a dog around. One day while I was at school and Harley was at the garage, my dad ran over her when moving one of the vehicles. They rushed her to the vet, and when I came home from school that day, my mom told me what happened.

Through all the emotion and tears, I somehow understood in my seven-year-old brain that the surgery she needed to save her life was going to be a lot of money—$660. And I also was able to figure out before they told me that it was money we didn't have. But I knew Harley needed that surgery, and I would do anything to help her. So I told my parents I'd get the money but to please get her the surgery.

In the garage office, we made coffee for the customers. I used to save the empty metal Folgers cans for my dad. He would use them to store nuts, bolts, or various parts in them. So I grabbed all the metal cans I could find, a roll of duct tape, and a black sharpie. I wrapped each can with duct tape and wrote "HARLEY'S FUND - Please help me save my dog." I took one can up to the parts store above my dad's garage. I took a second can to another parts store across town and left a third on the office desk at my dad's garage.

I didn't raise all of the $660, but I did raise $134. Thankfully my parents knew the vet and gave Dr. Caslow their word to make payments on the rest. Harley had her surgery and she lived for another 17 years.

She was there for me every day after school. She was there for me when kids were mean, she was there when I tripped over a part and when I smashed my knee on a motor that was being rebuilt. She was there when my heart was broken and when I was betrayed in my teens. She was there for me through my parents' almost divorce—and she was there for me again when they finally did. She knew things I never told another human, and her fur was the resting place for many of my tears.

Little did I know then that 18 years later, this experience I had with Harley when I was a young girl would be an emotional spark that led me to launch a major part of my life's purpose. I had never thought of starting a nonprofit or an animal shelter before that moment sitting in front of my empty building.

I have always loved animals. I feel it's our job to speak for those who can't and somehow I always saw myself in them. I wanted to help end, or at a minimum relieve, their suffering in some way. And although I never consciously thought of starting a nonprofit, instinctively, I always wanted to give back, to make a difference—and I know you do too.

Contribution Is the Key to Fulfillment

We live in a society filled with dreams of wealth, believing that money will bring happiness and success.

Yet we hear story after story after story about some of the richest, wealthiest, and financially successful people turning to drugs, alcohol, sex, or other addictions to numb their pain—and when that doesn't work, we hear the news stories of their suicides, from the millionaire who committed suicide on the front lawn of his $2.5 million home to the property tycoon who played polo with Prince Charles yet threw himself in front of a London Underground train.

So many people believe that when they get rich, they'll be happy. Yet we hear countless stories of those who—from the outside—"have it all" yet are addicted to drugs or alcohol, are depressed and feel lost, or filled with anger and rage. It begs the question, Why are so many rich people miserable? Why are there countless stories of millionaires who even turn to suicide?

The answer is clear: **Money doesn't buy fulfillment.**

> **Happiness isn't something external that others give you, it's something internal that you give yourself.**

You often hear the phrase "Money doesn't buy happiness," and it's true. Yes, money can buy a lot of things that will make you happy. Money can provide you with your dream house, the ability to move anywhere you want, pay off your parents' house, or travel the world.

But the tricky thing with that is happiness is temporary, fleeting. It doesn't matter if you achieved some big goal or accomplished some dream, the intensity of that feeling passes with time.

Most people think it's a state we can exist in forever, and when you aren't feeling happy, you think something is wrong with you. There isn't anything wrong with you not being happy all the time. Happiness is an emotion, it's fleeting. Fulfillment, on the other hand, isn't an emotion, it's deeper. Fulfillment lasts.

> **Happiness comes from *what* we do. Fulfillment comes from *why* we do it.**

We don't necessarily find happiness in our jobs every minute of every day, but we can feel fulfilled by our work every day if it makes us feel part of something bigger than ourselves. That's the reason we can feel unfulfilled even if we're successful by standard measures of compensation and status. You may find happiness when you land a big contract at work, but fulfillment only comes if you know you're contributing to a larger cause.

The six human needs are one of the greatest strategies for living a fulfilled life. I'm not going to go into it too much as there are many people and authors who talk about it, but just in case you aren't familiar, I'll summarize it here.

The concept of basic human needs was first introduced by Sigmund Freud. It was further developed by several psychologists over the years and most famously pulled together by Brooklyn-born American psychologist Abraham Maslow (Price, n.d.).

In more recent years, Tony Robbins adapted Maslow's theory and teachings into one of the greatest tools in existence for life transformation.

The premise is this: We all have needs, not just for basic survival, but six profound needs that must be fulfilled for a life of quality. The needs are:

1. Love/connection;
2. Variety;
3. Significance;
4. Certainty;
5. Growth;
6. Contribution.

It is said the first four needs are necessary for survival and a successful life, and the last two create a fulfilled life (Prince, n.d.). The first four can be tricky because you have to find balance in them; otherwise, you can find yourself in the position of those successful millionaires—all focused on success, fame, wealth (going after the high of significance and certainty) only to find yourself caught up in all the wrong things.

After studying these principles decades ago, and applying it into my own life for the last 25 years, I believe Maslow missed a connection inside of the six.

Because there is one, and only one, of the six basic human needs that he identified that can regulate any imbalances in the others. There is only one that can actually provide all of the other five. **That is contribution**.

Contribution Regulates and Provides All the Other Human Needs

Contribution provides:

Love/Connection   Contribution to a cause or charity you care about will provide connection and love that you can measure. I can't tell you how much love I receive from the animals in our care and how connected I feel to the mission and the people I serve with. Volunteering and giving back truly gives you far more than you'll ever be able to give the cause.

Certainty   Certainty is one of the human needs that can go awry. If left unbalanced, seeking certainty can lead to addictive or obsessive behaviors—such as power and control. By contributing beyond yourself, you are focused on activities that create healthy and empowering routines into your life and provides certainty in positive ways.

Variety   Contribution provides variety as you're typically learning something new, meeting new people, and doing something unique. It enables you to get out of the mundane to do something different outside of your everyday work and typical day-to-day routine.

Significance   Contribution provides significance because you realize you're making a difference by helping others. Those who don't have a positive way to feel significant may end up taking unhealthy measures to make themselves feel good, such as drugs, alcohol, or seeking validation. Contribution gives significance in a healthy way as you're often seen, recognized, and needed.

Growth   Contribution provides immense growth. As you contribute to others, there is a shift that occurs in your brain that radically shifts your perspective of life. You grow spiritually, mentally, and emotionally. You become more grateful, and that energy stacks up, acting as a magnet and drawing more miracles into your life.

Of course, as with most things, there are both positive and negative ways to contribute. It's the positive contributions where you will find your true value.

Positive Contribution:

- Volunteer work;
- Visiting nursing homes;
- Community service;
- Charitable donations;
- Adopting a child;

- Fostering dogs or children;
- Being a mentor;
- Being kind to others;
- Get involved in legislation to create positive change;
- Working in a field that creates positive impact.

Negative Contribution:

- Destroying others;
- Gossiping;
- Bullying;
- Spreading rumors;
- Being condescending.

Beyond What Contribution Does for You, It's Really About What You Can Do for Others

According to an article from the Cleveland Clinic, studies show that giving can actually boost your physical and mental health. Health benefits associated with giving are:

- Lower blood pressure;
- Increased self-esteem;
- Less depression;
- Lower stress levels;
- Longer life;
- Greater happiness and satisfaction.

I can remember getting a dollar for my allowance as a child and taking it to school to buy my parents a gift from Santa's Workshop. I was so excited to give them this little cheap janky gift at Christmas that I could barely wait for them to open it. The quality of the gift didn't matter—it was the idea of giving it that mattered the most. There's something about giving that makes us feel good, and there's actually science backing it up.

The Cleveland Clinic article continues on that research shows that people who give social support to others have lower blood pressure than people who don't. Supportive interaction with others also helps people recover from coronary-related events. Researchers also say that people who give their time to help others through community and organizational involvement have greater self-esteem, less depression, and lower stress levels than those who don't.

According to one study, people who were 55 and older who volunteered for two or more organizations were 44% less likely to die over a five-year period than those who didn't volunteer—***even*** accounting for many other factors including age, exercise, general health, and negative habits such as smoking!

Biologically, giving can create a "warm glow," activating regions in the brain associated with pleasure, connection with other people, and trust. This is the reason why you feel excitement when you're about to give a gift to someone else (and why you feel close to them while doing it) or why you feel happy driving home from a volunteer experience.

There is evidence that, during gift-giving behaviors, humans secrete "feel good" chemicals in our brains, such as serotonin (a mood-mediating chemical), dopamine (a feel-good chemical), and oxytocin (a compassion and bonding chemical).

When scientists looked at the fMRIs of subjects who gave to various charities, they found that giving stimulates the mesolimbic pathway, which is the reward center in the brain—releasing endorphins and creating what is known as the "helper's high." And like other highs, this one is addictive too, but in a positive way.

Decide what charities you'd like to give to, help, and support. Your mental and physical health will thank you—and so will those you help (Cleveland Clinic, 2020).

Giving can be a complex decision involving financial planning, personal values, and connection to others. And there are many ways to give.

You might create a donor-advised fund, give to one or multiple charities, give anonymously, or share your skills with a cause important to you. You can give together with friends, volunteer your time, or send charitable dollars to loved ones to name a few.

Knowing your own tendencies and traits can help identify ways of giving that will bring you satisfaction and joy. But here's the bottom-line: **You're here for a reason—isn't it time to find out why?**

I truly believe that every single one of us is here for a reason. We haven't been put here to just build a business, generate wealth, and die with a boat filled with cash. Giving, being a part of something that's bigger than yourself—that is really what makes "this" all matter.

Walk Toward That Which Breaks Your Heart

I started Heal Animal Rescue in 2006 with the sole goal to give back and make a difference. To help all of those animals, like my dog Harley, who were abandoned, abused, and left with nowhere to go.

Knowing the difficulty, energy, and focus it took to do what I did, I can say that starting a nonprofit was not a *smart* decision, it was a *heart* decision. But choosing to donate that building, serving as a volunteer for over 15 years—actively leading, growing, and overseeing financial operations including directing 62 charity events, planning and opening our second location, and raising millions of dollars for our mission of helping animals, all without ever taking a dime from the organization—has been one of the most difficult things I've done in my life yet equally the most rewarding.

Your Pain Is the Path toward Your Purpose

But when I look back I have to ask, do you think I would have such a heart for abused animals, or have so much empathy for their pain, if I didn't experience abuse as a child? Do you think I would be so passionate about being a voice for others, if I didn't know the feeling of being silenced as a little girl? Often, we avoid addressing the pain in our lives. Perhaps we bury the trauma, get angry about what has happened, or look for someone to hate and blame. But your greatest adversities, your greatest struggles, your greatest pain, can plant seeds to your greatest purpose. The strongest people have been through the greatest challenges because just like steel, our strength is forged in the fire. I think back and smile at all the different times I would wake up super early to work on a project, work 18 to 20 hours a day without issue—and every one of them was for something that I got paid nothing to do.

It was when I worked on an animal cruelty case and we got the longest time served for animal cruelty in Pennsylvania at that time.

It was the time I found out another shelter was being shut down by the state and 67 animals were going to be euthanized. In five days, I led an army of volunteers and turned an entire vacant building I owned into a temporary shelter to save all of them from being killed.

It is the moments like these that I remember the most. Seeing all the little faces of those we saved, and seeing how one decision pulled so many people together to accomplish one goal. It was these moments that made my days beyond full, yet my time was well served—not the times I was trying to meet a sales goal for the first quarter. Your circumstances, your past, does not define you. You cannot control what was done *to* you, but you do have the power to control what you do next.

Now I serve in a less active role on the board but still have my hands in giving back to numerous charities and causes important to me. Because I know how contribution not only provides all the other human needs, but it helped me *heal*. And I know it can do the same for you.

The key to fulfillment and richness of life is not the accumulation of wealth, it is the contribution of what you can do with it.

How you contribute, and how you give, is going to look completely different than how I contribute or how anyone else does. But just like you picked up this book with a decision to build your wealth habits, make that same decision about contribution.

If you want to start or you've been so focused on creating more wealth for yourself that you haven't even thought of contributing, I'm going to ask you a question:

I want you to imagine you have $100 million in the bank. Right now, $100,000,000 sits in a bank account with your name on it but you can't touch it unless you follow this one rule:

$100 Million Dollar Rule

The only way you could withdraw any of the money is you have to work. Six hours a day. Six days a week. Every week for the next 20 years. And as long as you did, you would be able to withdraw that $100 million.

What would you do?

_____

_____

_____

When money is taken off the table as a need or desire and *contribution* is the only driving factor of our life, we begin to see things that we may have been blinded to all along.

But regardless of where you are right now on your journey to building wealth, you can start contributing today by using the 10 × 3 Rule.

10 × 3 Rule

Decide to contribute today by following the 10/10/10 guideline:

10% of your money;
10% of your time; and
10% of your wealth.

10% of your income—donate to a cause or mission you care about.
10% of your time—volunteer with an organization that's important to you.
10% of your wealth—bequest it to a charity or nonprofit upon your death.

Become a part of something bigger than yourself, and watch how your life will change.

Contribution isn't some fluffy line or talking point. It is really what life's all about. And it really is why we are all really here.

Here are a few of my favorite 501c3 nonprofits:

Heal Animal Rescue
www.HealAnimalRescue.org

Liberty Wildlife
www.LibertyWildlife.org

Love Them All
www.LoveThemAllRescue.org

Where True Wealth Lives

It's hard to believe we have reached the end of this journey together. And although this is just the beginning in many ways, it's an incredible start toward you creating financial freedom.

You've already accomplished what most people don't—you made a decision and took the steps to build a better financial future for yourself and your family. I am very proud of you for the commitment you've made and dedication you have to see it through.

Before we go, I have one more thing to share and one final question to ask.

As you start to apply the *wealth habits* covered throughout this book, as you begin your ascent to more wealth, and as you take control of your financial future, please do not forget what matters most.

Celebrating friendships, spending time with family, being with those you love, helping others, deepening your spiritual relationship, serving missions and causes that are doing good work—giving—that's the real reason to create wealth. It's to have more time, to create more experiences—to *give more*.

The contributions you make—that's what will create more wealth than you can measure. When you shift from a place of "what can I get" and replace it with the belief of "what can I give," life starts to make sense.

You can build all the *wealth habits* discussed in this book, but if you miss this one, the final *wealth habit*, you won't build true wealth, *real* wealth, the wealth that extends through all the others.

So I am going to ask you the most important question of them all: **What will be your contribution?**

_____
_____
_____
_____
_____

Signed: _____ Today's date: _____

Resources and References

Aaron, M. (2018). "Why 'start with why' is bad advice." That Seems Important (March 15). https://www.thatseemsimportant.com/branding/start-with-why-is-bad-advice/.

Baldridge, R. (2022). "Best retirement plans for small businesses in 2022." Inc. (August 16). https://www.inc.com/hr-outsourcing/best-retirement-plans-for-small-businesses.html.

Bond, C. (2022). "Indexed universal life insurance explained." Forbes Advisor (May 10). https://www.forbes.com/advisor/life-insurance/indexed-universal-life-insurance/.

Castrillon, C. (n.d.) "How to shift from a scarcity to a abundance mindset." Corporate Escape Artist blog. https://corporateescapeartist.com/shift-from-scarcity-to-abundance-mindset/.

Choicehacking.com. "Why Steve Jobs stole from a hotel to build the first Apple store (and you should too)." https://www.choicehacking.com/2022/08/01/apple-store-ritz-carlton-psychology/.

Chowdhury, M.R. (2019). "The neuroscience of gratitude and how it affects anxiety & grief." Positive Psychology (April 9). https://positivepsychology.com/neuroscience-of-gratitude/#:~:text=When%20we%20express%20gratitude%20and,feel%20happy%20from%20the%20inside.

Clark, A.H. (n.d.). "The commodity of attention and the challenge of staying focused." Clark Psychology Group. https://aliciaclarkpsyd.com/commodity-of-attention/.

Clear, J. (n.d.). "Successful people start before they feel ready." https://jamesclear.com/successful-people-start-before-they-feel-ready.

Cleveland Clinic, 2020. "Why giving is good for your health." (October 28). https://health.clevelandclinic.org/why-giving-is-good-for-your-health/.

Crowley, J. (2011). "10 millionaire businessmen who committed suicide." Business Pundit (November 30). https://www.businesspundit.com/10-millionaire-businessmen-who-committed-suicide/.

Dave, P. (2021). "Variable life vs. variable universal: what's the difference?" Investopedia (August 31). https://www.investopedia.com/articles/pf/07/variable_universal.asp.

Davis, G.B. (2022). "The BRRRR method: real estate leverage with 100% financing (infographic)." Spark Rental (March 16). https://sparkrental.com/brrrr-method-real-estate-leverage/.

Doherty, L. (2017). "The science behind vision boards." The Motivation Clinic blog. https://www.themotivationclinic.co.uk/blog/blog-post-title-three-grwe9#:~:text=Neuroscientist%20Dr%20Tara%20Swart%20explains,and%20filters%20out%20unnecessary%20information.%E2%80%9D

de Ruijter, J. (n.d.). "Solutions-focused thinking." Hat Rabbits. https://hatrabbits.com/en/solutions-focused-thinking/.

Dividends Diversify. (n.d.). "Examples of portfolio income & 10+ ways to increase it." https://dividendsdiversify.com/examples-of-portfolio-income/.

Elkins, K. (2017). "Self-made millionaires say you should think twice before going to colleage." Make It article, CNBC.com (July 11). https://www.cnbc.com/2017/07/11/self-made-millionaires-dont-go-to-college.html.

Ellsberg, M. (2011). *The Education of Millionaires: Everything You Won't Learn in College About How to Be Successful.* New York: Portfolio.

Fahrenkopf, E., Guo, J., and Argote, L. (2020). "Personnel mobility and organizational performance: The effects of specialist vs. generalist experience and organizational work structure." *Organization Science* 31(6): 1601–1620.

Finn, E.S. et al. (2015). "Functional connectome fingerprinting: identifying individuals using patterns of brain connectivity," *Nature Neuroscience* 18(11).

Fontinelle, A. (2021). "7 situations where a trust might help." Mass Mutual blog (January 12). https://blog.massmutual.com/post/trust-situations.

Fontinelle, A. (2021). "How umbrella insurance works." Investopedia (June 8). https://www.investopedia.com/articles/personal-finance/040115/how-umbrella-insurance-works.asp.

Frank, R. (2022). "Soaring markets helped the richest 1% gain $6.5 trillion in wealth last year, according to the Fed." CNBC.com (April 1). https://www.cnbc.com/2022/04/01/richest-one-percent-gained-trillions-in-wealth-2021.html.

Gariepy, L. (2022). "Tax benefits of real estate investing: top 6 breaks and deductions." Rocket Mortgage (July 7). https://www.rocketmortgage.com/learn/tax-benefits-of-real-estate-investing.

Gourguechon, P. (2019). "The psychology of money: what you really need to know to have a (relatively) fearless financial life." *Forbes* (February 25). https://www.forbes.com/sites/prudygourguechon/2019/02/25/the-psychology-of-money-what-you-need-to-know-to-have-a-relatively-fearless-financial-life/?sh=2a70066adfe8.

Greene, D. (n.d.). "How to succeed in real estate investing using the BRRRR method." Bigger Pockets. https://www.biggerpockets.com/guides/brrrr-method.

Hayes, A. (2022). "Bond fund." Investopedia (April 18). https://www.investopedia.com/terms/b/bondfund.asp#:~:text=A%20bond%20fund%2C%20also%20referred,generating%20monthly%20income%20for%20investors.

Health Essentials. (2020). "Why giving is good for your health." Cleveland Clinic (October 28). https://health.clevelandclinic.org/why-giving-is-good-for-your-health/.

Hendricks, D. (n.d.) "8 reasons business plans fail that no one wants to talk about. Bplans." https://articles.bplans.com/8-reasons-business-plans-fail-that-no-one-wants-to-talk-about/.

Hess, A.J. (2018). "Stanford researchers: 'Follow your passion' advice could make you less successsful." Make it article. https://www.cnbc.com/2018/06/22/stanford-researchers-following-your-passion-makes-you-less-successful.html.

Irafinancialgroup.com. 2022 Solo 401(k) contribution rules. (January 5). https://www.irafinancialgroup.com/learn-more/solo-401k/2022-solo-401k-contribution-rules/

Jahnke, T. (2022). "What is real estate cash flow and how do you maximize it?" roofstock.com (March 10). https://learn.roofstock.com/blog/real-estate-cash-flow.

Johnson, H. (2021). "Best universal life insurance companies." Investopedia (November 13). https://www.investopedia.com/best-universal-life-insurance-4845846.

Josephson, A. (2022). "Understanding how your taxes work." Smart Asset (January 5). https://smartasset.com/taxes/understanding-taxes.

Kagan, J. (2021). "Equity-indexed universal life insurance." Investopedia (February 12). https://www.investopedia.com/terms/e/equity-indexed-universal-life-nsurance.asp.

Kagan, J. (2021). "Key person insurance." Investopedia (July 27). https://www.investo pedia.com/terms/k/keypersoninsurance.asp#:~:text=Key%20person%20insur ance%20is%20a%20life%20insurance%20policy%20a%20company,be%20the%20 owner%20or%20founder.

Kagan, J. (2022). "Self-Employed Contributions Act (SECA) Tax." Investopedia (April 7). https://www.investopedia.com/terms/s/seca.asp.

Kalfrin, V. and Rogacz, C. (2022). "What upgrades increase home value? 25 high-ROI improvements buyers love." homelight.com (January 31). https://www.homelight. com/blog/what-upgrades-increase-home-value/.

Kilroy, A. (2022). "Permanent life insurance explained." Forbes Advisor (May 12). https://www.forbes.com/advisor/life-insurance/permanent/.

Kuepper, J. (2022). "Indexed universal life insurance: pros and cons." Investopedia (March 2). https://www.investopedia.com/articles/personal-finance/012416/pros- and-cons-indexed-universal-life-insurance.asp.

Lahunou, I. (2022). "8 ways to increase purchase frequency." Monetha (April 26). https://www.monetha.io/blog/customer-loyalty/purchase-frequency/.

Landon, D. (n.d.) "The top 10 metrics every real estate investor should know (and why)." www.stessa.com. https://www.stessa.com/blog/10-real-estate-investing-metrics/.

La Roche, J. (2021). "Charlie Munger: It's 'absolute insanity' to think owning 100 stocks instead of five makes you a better investor." Yahoo!Finance (February 25). https://www.yahoo.com/video/charlie-munger-on-value-investing-and-the-crisis- in-wealth-management-114327424.html?guccounter=1&guce_referrer=aHR 0cHM6Ly93d3cuZ29vZ2xlLmNvbS8&guce_referrer_sig=AQAAAHug4M-zi6 ShTtR9kVxh1QY2p7QZ0-BxkSu93kEm6D2XpoGgqTsSUz3mjV8AaLGgXSAAVW Ze2W7Mesb5f3dAr5OIK09wp06P-7iaqdxH9dVFwajf9pQLKyqu-itj31emZATtW6q U7p92qPIti8nWcxCVWjhX1n_Mna0qOkkhJiuk#:~:text=Munger%20observed%20 that%20in%20the,Absolute%20insanity%2C%E2%80%9D%20Munger%20said.

Lazarony, L. (2021). "Types of small business insurance." Forbes Advisor (October 11). https://www.forbes.com/advisor/business-insurance/types-of-small-business- insurance/.

Leefeldt, E. (2022). "Sounding the alarm on indexed universal life insurance." Forbes Advisor (July 28). https://www.forbes.com/advisor/life-insurance/indexed- universal-life-insurance-problems/.

Luest, H. (n.d.) "Connection—the key to healing and resilience." *The New Social Worker*. https://www.socialworker.com/feature-articles/practice/connection-key-to- healing-resilience/#:~:text=While%20recognizing%20the%20space%20and, understand%20our%20feelings%20and%20experiences.

Mann, B. (2022). "7 key ratios every real estate investor should know." The Smart Inves- tor (May 4). https://thesmartinvestor.com/investing/real-estate/real-estate-investor- ratios/#:~:text=Here's%20a%20sample%20computation%3A%20If,1%25%20would% 20be%20good%20enough.

MasterClass. (2022). "What is customer acquisition? Customer acquisition explained." www.masterclass.com. https://www.masterclass.com/articles/customer-acquisition.

Merelli, A. (2022). "The pandemic created a new billionaire every 30 hours." Quartz (July 30). https://qz.com/2168839/the-pandemic-created-almost-600-new-billi onaires/.

Metz, J. (2022). "How to get directors and officers insurance." Forbes Advisor (May 16). https://www.forbes.com/advisor/business-insurance/directors-and-officers-insurance/

Morin, C. (2019). "How the Ritz-Carlton creates a 5 star customer experience." CRM.org (December 13). https://crm.org/articles/ritz-carlton-gold-standards#:~:text=One%20 Ritz%2DCarlton's%20service%20values,employees%20with%20decision%2Dmaking%20 authority.

Price, J. (n.d.). "The 6 human needs." https://www.jenniferprice.com/post/2016/09/20/ the-greatest-strategy-6-basic-human-needs#:~:text=The%20needs%20are%3A%20 Love%2FConnection,Certainty%2C%20Growth%2C%20and%20Contribution.

Rohde, J. (n.d.). "Common rental property expenses & which ones are deductible." https://www.stessa.com/blog/rental-property-expenses/.

Safane, J. (2022). "What are ordinary and necessary expenses?" The Balance (April 25). https://www.thebalancemoney.com/what-are-ordinary-and-necessary-expenses-5218671#:~:text=Ordinary%20and%20necessary%20expenses%20are,part%20of%20 determining%20taxable%20income.

Savage, S. (2015). "Entitlement is stealing our future." Thin Difference (May 5). https:// www.thindifference.com/2015/05/entitlement-is-stealing-our-future/.

Schramm, S. (2021). "3 ways to bounce back after a work interruption." *Duke Today* (November 30). https://today.duke.edu/2021/11/3-ways-bounce-back-after-work-interruption.

Scott, J. (n.d.). "How to be a flexible investor & profit in any real estate market." Coach Carson. https://www.coachcarson.com/flexible-real-estate-investor-profit-any-market/.

Sinek, S. (2017). "What's the difference between fulfillment and happiness." LinkedIn (September 2). https://www.linkedin.com/pulse/whats-difference-between-fulfillment-happiness-simon-sinek/.

Sinrich, J. (2021). "28 amazing facts about your brain that will blow your mind." The Healthy (March 31). https://www.thehealthy.com/aging/mind-memory/brain-facts/.

Smith, L. (2021). "8 fund types to use in a recession." Investopedia (October 13). https:// www.investopedia.com/articles/mutualfund/08/recession-proof-mutual-funds.asp.

Smith, L. (2022). "How to increase your real estate net worth with leveraging." Investopedia (June 4). https://www.investopedia.com/articles/mortgages-real-estate/10/ increase-your-real-estate-net-worth.asp.

Stewart, J. (2022). "Roth IRA contribution limits for 2022." Kiplinger (May 20). https://www.kiplinger.com/retirement/retirement-plans/roth-iras/603954/roth-ira-contribution-limits-for-2022.

Stinson, N. (2019). "10 steps to develop an abundance mindset." www.chopra.com, https://chopra.com/articles/10-steps-to-develop-an-abundance-mindset.

Team Tony. (n.d.). "Discover the 6 human needs: these core needs drive every decision you make." tonyrobbins.com. https://www.tonyrobbins.com/mind-meaning/ do-you-need-to-feel-significant/.

Team Tony. (n.d.) "Are You Free of Financial Fear?" Above Whispers.com podcast. http://abovewhispers.com/2017/01/10/free-financial-fear-2/.

The Investopedia Team. (2022). "7 ways to recession-proof your life." Investopedia (June 24). https://www.investopedia.com/articles/pf/08/recession-proof-your-life .asp#:~:text=If%20you%20make%20it%20a,in%20other%20areas%20to%20 compensate.

The Productive Engineer blog. "Hardest or easiest work first? What the research shows," https://theproductiveengineer.net/hardest-or-easiest-work-first-what-the-research-shows/

The Ritz Carlton. (n.d.) "Gold Standards." https://www.ritzcarlton.com/en/about/gold-standards.

Tidgren, K.A. (2018). "Corporate veil pierced where owner was sloppy with finances." Ag Docket (August 30). https://www.calt.iastate.edu/blogpost/corporate-veil-pierced-where-owner-was-sloppy-finances.

Uber, M., and Attardo, P. (2021). "Remodeling? Avoid these 10 home improvements that do not add value." Homelight (January 29). https://www.homelight.com/blog/home-improvements-that-do-not-add-value/.

U.S. News & World Report. (2022). "9 red flags that could trigger a tax audit." WTOP news (February 21). https://wtop.com/government/2022/02/9-red-flags-that-could-trigger-a-tax-audit/.

Warrell, M. (2019). "Does money cause you stress? The unconscious money beliefs keeping you from a richer life." *Forbes* (August 9). https://www.forbes.com/sites/margiewarrell/2019/08/09/money-making-you-stressed-the-unconscious-money-beliefs-keeping-you-from-a-richer-life/.

Waschenfelder, T. (n.d.). "Play the long game: delay gratification now to get more later." Wealest. https://www.wealest.com/articles/long-game.

Weintraub, K. (2019). "The adult brain does grow new neurons after all, study says." *Scientific American* (March 25). https://www.scientificamerican.com/article/the-adult-brain-does-grow-new-neurons-after-all-study-says/.

Wells Fargo. (2021). "Qualified opportunity zones: what investors should know." (August). https://www.wellsfargo.com/the-private-bank/insights/planning/wpu-qualified-opportunity-zones/#:~:text=The%20Opportunity%20Zone%20program%20allows,property%20to%20defer%20the%20gain.

Wells, S. (n.d.). "The importance of 'showing up.'" Thrive Global. https://thriveglobal.com/stories/the-importance-of-showing-up/#:~:text=It's%20about%20appearing%20consistently%20for,one%20day%20at%20a%20time.

Wuench, J. (2021). "Follow your passion is the worst career advice—here's why." *Forbes* (May 19). https://www.forbes.com/sites/juliawuench/2021/05/19/follow-your-passion-is-the-worst-career-advice-heres-why/?sh=dbd24cd22d43.

Yale, A.J. (2022). "What to know about the scarcity mindset and how it affects women and their finances—and 6 ways to avoid it." Insider (March 7). https://www2.businessinsider.com/personal-finance/scarcity-mindset.

Acknowledgments

I just completed the last page of the manuscript, and I feel so incredibly blessed to sit and write these acknowledgments.

There have been so many people who have inspired me, encouraged me, and supported me. I will never be able to list them all but I have to start with Who it all starts with—God. Thank you for guiding me during all of the challenging times in my life. Thank you for your voice, for your protection, and your reassurance. Thank you for laying this book on my heart and giving me the courage to write it. I am immensely grateful for Your grace and the gift of this life.

Thank you to Daniel Decker for seeing something special in me and for masterfully orchestrating the book launch. You were the first domino for this book and I am so grateful for your friendship.

To Shannon Vargo, Sally Baker, and the incredible team at Wiley for believing in me and this book, and for taking me into the Wiley family. A special thanks to Julie Kerr for carefully editing this manuscript and for being so kind and patient with this rookie author. And to the Wiley team who copyedited and typeset my words and turned them into this incredible book.

To Tony Robbins, if I hadn't found you and your cassette tapes when I was a teenager, I have no idea how my life would look. I am forever grateful for you and those 3 a.m. infomercials.☺ You were a mentor long before you ever knew who I was. I am grateful for your presence and thank you for being a cornerstone in my life. To Brendon Burchard, thank you for your being a bright light during one of the most difficult times in my life. Your talents and example in this industry have been invaluable and I appreciate you so much. To my friends in the industry, Rory and AJ Vaden, Jon and Kathryn Gordon, Lewis Howes, Michael Ellsberg, and so many others, thank you for all of your encouragement and support—this wouldn't be what it is without you.

To the authors of the books that I learned so much from—David Bach, Thomas J. Stanley, Napoleon Hill, David J. Schwartz—your words gave this once uneducated kid an invaluable self-education. Thank you for sharing your wisdom with the world.

Kel and Kimmie—two of my closest friends since high school—thank you for your lifelong friendship, endless laughs, and sister-like love. To my friend Anne Degre who passed away before her time. Thank you for your example of strength and for showing me how to be unapologetic as a female in business. I miss you dearly.

To all the rescue dogs who have given me so much unconditional love along the way. Louie, Mia, Henry, Gucci, Carlos, Gianni, Winston, and the rest of the pack—you have taught me so much, given me so much joy and truly rescued me.

The team and board at Heal Animal Rescue, thank you for your dedication to being a voice for the animals. A special thanks to Bethany Morse and Jessica Rafferty for your continued friendship, loyalty, and commitment to our mission.

To my team and clients all over the world, thank you for giving me this incredible opportunity, and for accepting my gritty, hard-hitting education with love. I am grateful to each of you for giving me the joy of watching you succeed, I am continually cheering you on.

To my dad, thank you for your continued example of strength, hard work, and for showing me how to never give up. Thank you for always being there for me—regardless of the challenge, and for reminding me to never care about what people think. And to my mom, for having me when she was 16 when she could have very easily not. Thank you for always being willing to help, to lend a hand, and be there for me whenever and wherever needed.

Last but certainly not least, Anthony. Thank you for always making me laugh, for your strength in the storms and for always believing in me. Every year together brings more excitement, greater adventure, and a deeper love. Thank you for your continued encouragement, for your support, and for loving me—for who I am, and for who I'm not.

To you the reader, and everyone who has supported this book, thank you does not begin to describe my gratitude for you.

Much love,
Candy

About the Author

Candy Valentino built her first multi-million-dollar business before she could legally order a drink.

At 19 years old with no degree, no corporate background, and no money, she founded, scaled, and successfully sold businesses in service, retail, e-commerce, and product manufacturing in addition to creating a vast real estate portfolio as a flipper and investor.

Through her success in business, at the age of 26, Candy founded a non-profit charity. She bought and donated a building to the organization and since then they have gone on to save thousands of animals. She has been actively involved for more than 15 years, personally raising millions.

During her two-and-a-half decades as an entrepreneur she has been named to Top Business Leaders 40 Under 40, Top 50 Women In Business, 10 People Making a Difference, Top 10 Business Consultants by Yahoo Finance, and was the youngest female to receive the Governor's Award in Entrepreneurship in Pennsylvania. *SUCCESS* magazine named her "Women of Influence," as well as "Leaders Who Get Results" with names like Tony Robbins, and Brene Brown.

She's been featured in numerous TV, radio, magazine, and newspaper articles—not only for business and investing, but for her advocacy and philanthropic work. She was named "Person of Distinction" in Arizona.

After the exit of her last company, Candy started sharing her gritty, real-world business and investing strategies online, gathering an audience of millions. Leveraging almost 25 years of experience amassed from creating successful businesses in multiple industries, and generating wealth through REI, Candy is an author, speaker, and trainer on the topics of wealth creation, business development, and real estate investing.

www.candyvalentino.com
Socials: FB, IG, TikTok @candyvalentino

Index